Was this Camelot?

NEW ASPECTS OF ARCHAEOLOGY

Edited by Sir Mortimer Wheeler

Was this Camelot?

Excavations at Cadbury Castle 1966-1970

Leslie Alcock

15 Color Plates
95 Monochrome Plates
36 Line Drawings

STEIN AND DAY,

PUBLISHERS, NEW YORK

To

D V C   D M E   H S G

C L   C R M   M G S

whose skill and dedication ensured the success of
the Cadbury–Camelot enterprise

First published in the United States in 1972
This edition © Thames and Hudson 1972
Library of Congress Catalog No. 72-82214
All Rights Reserved

Printed and bound in Great Britain by
Hazell Watson and Viney Ltd, Aylesbury
Stein and Day, Publisher, 7 East 48 Street, New York, N.Y. 100017

ISBN *8128-1505-x*

Contents

General Editor's Preface

I have no hesitation in presenting this book on a personal note. In 1950, after war-experience in India, Mr Leslie Alcock decided to attach himself to me during a part of my term as an adviser to the then-new Pakistan government. At the time my functions included the training of new or potential attachés to the recently established Pakistan Department of Archaeology, and I was delighted to have my hand strengthened by this new Oxford volunteer. Thereafter at Mohenjo-daro, one of the two principal sites of the ancient Indus Civilization, he was my chief colleague as an instructor at an archaeological training-school. His tireless work in that capacity was invaluable to Pakistan and incidentally to me, with many other tasks and diversions upon my table.

When therefore, years later after productive work by Alcock on several sites in Wales, I was invited to the formal presidency of a committee established for the patronage of a proposed excavation of Cadbury-Camelot in Somerset under his direction, I accepted with pleasure and alacrity. I did so also with some anticipation of the rather special problems which were likely to be involved. Plainly enough the site, then known as Cadbury Castle, was a substantial multivallate hillfort of manageable area. Equally plainly, that was not the main or only reason for its choice as the scene of a major and certainly costly excavation. In the days of Leland and Camden, in the sixteenth century, the place had been associated with 'King' Arthur, in particular as Camelot, Arthur's supposititious capital. And now it was a visitor's chance discovery on the hilltop of pottery already recognized elsewhere by Dr Ralegh Radford as a Mediterranean product of plus/minus AD 500 that gave this discredited tradition a new verisimilitude. Of the Arthurian period we were singularly – almost resistantly – ignorant in any factual and material sense; but here at last was a possibility of something approaching chapter and verse. Stated otherwise, the substantive Iron Age hillfort was a firm base for all to see; on a minimum estimate, excavation here could not utterly fail; but now there was a real likelihood also of a positive advance upon new lines into the alluring crepuscular land of speculation where history and romance had long fought for possession.

In the event, the exploration has provided more than one bonus as it has proceeded. Beneath the prehistoric Iron Age lurks a Neolithic occupation some 5000 years old, and a Late Bronze Age of the eighth or seventh century BC. Over it a Roman task-force has scattered its *disjecta* from the time of the conquest of these westlands. Then there is now at last an indubitable 'Arthur' or his ilk. And, five centuries after his shadowy but persistent shape had on any showing passed from the scene, late 'Saxon' kings seemingly struck coins there and surrounded their mint with a solid mortared wall. In half-a-dozen directions the site has offered rich rewards to Alcock and his colleagues, and has incidentally made kindly nonsense of those earnest scholars who, desperately anxious to preserve their scientific integrity from Arthurian pollution, hesitated to approve a serious venture amidst the half-memories which are happily an occasional and often decorative part of historic humanism. Let these young critics, bless them, in this sort of context recall the epic battles and victories of Troy long ago, and of a certain Heinrich Schliemann who was not afraid so to venture. . . .

Certainly, Mr Alcock has throughout this complex operation thought clearly and soberly of the problems and evidences which he and his devoted team have encountered in five seasons of arduous and impeccable digging. In the following pages the entertaining results are displayed for us in a balanced summary, which includes a clear exposition of the aims and methods governing procedure from stage to stage. The unspecialized reader can thus not merely appreciate the main conclusions but can, it is hoped, in some real measure participate in the reasoned processes of discovery.

MORTIMER WHEELER

Foreword

This book is written for the enthusiasts who came, in tens of thousands, to see the excavation of Cadbury Castle; and for everyone like them, with no special knowledge but a lively interest in Arthur, in archaeology, or in history. It attempts to answer the kind of questions which they asked then, or have since asked my colleagues and myself when we have talked about Cadbury to non-specialist audiences.

One of the commonest of these questions is 'How do you know where to dig?' So in Part One I have tried to show how and why the excavation was organized, how policy was decided, and how, step by logical step, we expanded our knowledge. Inevitably, the story is a complicated one, because on an excavation of this size the making of decisions is necessarily a complex process.

In Part Two I sketch the results of the excavation as they appear at the present stage of research. This is in every sense a summary and interim report, but the analysis of finds and structures has already proceeded far enough for me to be confident that the outlines of the picture are firm.

The formal dedication is to the supervisors who held responsibility in the first season. They effectively ensured success in 1966, and laid a sound foundation for subsequent seasons. In addition to their role in 1966, they stand here as representatives not only of the supervisory staff of all five seasons, but of all my workers. I hope they will find that the results set out in Part Two are not unworthy of their efforts.

Even in the briefest of accounts, a few other specific acknowledgements must be made. First and foremost, a warm tribute is due to Mr and Mrs Montgomery, the owners of Cadbury Castle, for allowing the excavations: an inhabitant of South Cadbury might say, 'for suffering them'. Then to the officers of the Camelot Research Committee: to Sir Mortimer Wheeler for his stimulating Presidency; to Dr Ralegh Radford and Professor Sheppard Frere, for their wise guidance as successive Chairmen; to R. T. Brooks and S. C. Morland for the care which each in his own way devoted to our finances; and not least to our Secretary, Geoffrey Ashe, whose work was no less vital than that of the archaeologists, but far less exciting.

The typescript of the book has benefited from the criticisms of Elizabeth Alcock, Michael Bishop, Leonard Hayward and Chris Musson, and above all from the searching comments of Peter Crew. In seeing it into print I have been helped by the wise guidance of Peter Clayton, who has also provided illustrations. Finally, I wish to record my debt to the Department of Archaeology of University College, Cardiff. Without the facilities and resources so lavishly provided by that Department, neither this book, nor the research and exploration on which it was based, could have been undertaken.

I   The growth of a theory

Leland and the identification of Cadbury as Camelot

'At the very south ende of the chirch of South-Cadbyri standith Camallate, sumtyme a famose toun or castelle, apon a very torre or hille, wunderfully enstrengtheid of nature. In the upper parte of the coppe of the hille be 4. diches or trenches, and a balky waulle of yerth betwixt every one of them . . . Much gold, sylver and coper of the Romaine coynes hath be found ther yn plouing . . . The people can telle nothing ther but that they have hard say that Arture much resortid to Camalat'.

Thus wrote John Leland, self-styled King's Antiquary to Henry VIII, in 1542.[1] Leland was the first, and by no means the least, of a great line of British antiquaries and topographers. His sharp observations still have value today. But when the subject demanded, he could write in a more lyrical vein, as witness the account of Camelot in his *Assertion of Arthur*: 'Good Lorde, what and howe many most deepe Ditches are there heere? How many vallyes are there heere out of the earth delved? Againe what daungerous steepenesse? And to end in fewe wordes, truly me seemeth it is a mirackle, both in Arte and nature'.[2]

Today, Leland's Camalat appears as a steep-sided, free-standing hill with a grassy summit ridge rising above wooded flanks. Only at the south-east corner, and along part of the southern side, are some of its ancient fortifications visible above the trees. In the early eighteenth century, as William Stukeley's drawing so clearly reveals,[3] the ramparts had not yet been hidden by timber; and without a doubt they were similarly unencumbered in Leland's day. It is difficult for us now to imagine what Cadbury looked like then, but in 1967 an attempt was made to capture the visual effect by means of a model of the hill-top and its defences. The majesty of the original was inevitably lost in a model. Nevertheless, it was obvious that beneath its tree-cover, Cadbury Castle has few equals among British hillforts for the number, complexity, and above all the towering steepness of its defences. Leland's description, as we now see, was by no means over-dramatic.

Plates 1, 26, I, VII
Fig. 4

Plate 2

Plate 3

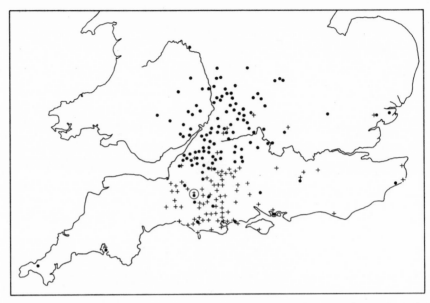

1 *The Iron Age background of Cadbury Castle (in circle). Coins of the Durotriges* + ; *and of the Dobunni* ●. *Based on the Ordnance Survey* Map of Southern Britain in the Iron Age

So much for the objective aspect of what Leland had seen in terms of substantial earthwork: what, then, of Arthur and Camelot? Here two quite different sets of questions are involved. First: was Leland reporting traditions about Cadbury which he found already present in the folk-lore of the region; or was he making attributions and identifications of his own? Second: what historical reality might lie behind such folk-lore or such identifications? Had there ever been a place like Camelot, or a man like the Arthur of the romances?

So far as the first set of questions goes, there is some evidence that Leland himself was responsible for the identification of Cadbury with Camelot, and that this owed nothing to local or popular tradition. Almost two centuries after Leland's visit, Stukeley, in his account of Camelot, reports that 'the country people are ignorant of this name, which has generally obtained among the learned',[4] and he recommends intending visitors to enquire for Cadbury Castle. Moreover, we know that Leland twisted the evidence – whether consciously or not – in support of his identification. He claimed that the name Camalat was still borne by such nearby villages 'as Quene-Camallat'. But that village, and its neighbour West Camel, have been Camelle, Cammell or plain Camel for at least nine hundred years, as the record of Domesday Book demonstrates. It is of course likely that it was the

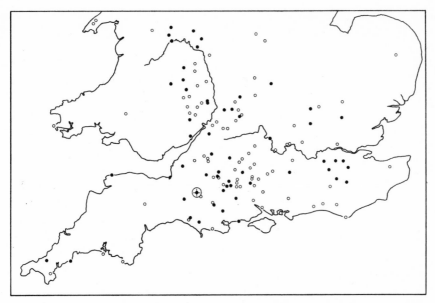

2 The Iron Age background of Cadbury Castle (in circle). Hillforts enclosing over 15 acres. Single rampart o; multiple ramparts ●. Based on the Ordnance Survey Map of Southern Britain in the Iron Age

Camel names, combined with the sight of the great fortifications, which put the idea of Camelot into Leland's mind. We can, indeed, have no confidence that he had received the identification from local informants.

The Arthurian attribution is another matter altogether. Leland is clearly recording what he had heard, not fabricating tales himself, when he reports the finding of a silver horseshoe within the camp. There is perhaps nothing necessarily Arthurian about this, but it shows the special character of the hill in contemporary folk-lore, and at some point, silver horseshoes came to be attributed to King Arthur and his knights in their ghostly ride around the hill at full moon. Moreover, the Welsh chronicler Elis Gruffydd, a contemporary of Leland, refers to a hill near Glastonbury which contains a cave where Arthur was said to lie sleeping.[5] Gruffydd does not identify the place more closely, but the nearest hill to Glastonbury, the Tor, has no sleeping-king associations. Cadbury, on the other hand, is certainly one of the places where Arthur is supposed to sleep, a belief inspired by a geological formation which suggests the presence of caverns. So it is a likely candidate for the hill mentioned by Gruffydd.

However that may be, it is certain that before the end of the sixteenth century strong Arthurian traditions were attached to the hill. William Camden, in his *Britannia*, reports that 'the local people call it Arthur's

Palace', *incolae Arthuri Palatium dicunt.*[6] This, it will be observed, is in direct conflict with what Stukeley wrote a century and a half later about the country-folk. But Camden's record deserves all the more credence because he did not believe for one moment in Arthur's Palace. 'It is, however', he roundly declares, 'a Roman work, as is shown by the coins that are dug up daily'.

In sum, then, there is a good case that Cadbury Castle already had Arthurian associations in Leland's day quite independent of his attribution. But he is probably responsible for the identification with Camelot. If we read his own words carefully and critically, this is in agreement with them. For he never says that the local people told him that the place was Camelot, only that 'they have hard say that Arture much resortid to Camalat'. This would have been true wherever Camelot was thought to be.

The authenticity of Arthur and Camelot

We come now to our second set of questions, those which have to do with the historical reality of Arthur and Camelot. It is as well to say outright that Camelot has no historical authenticity: it is a place that never was. The basis for this assertion is that it is not mentioned in the earliest traditions and earliest evidence about Arthur. In the twelfth century Geoffrey of Monmouth, in his *History of the Kings of Britain*, set Arthur's principal court in the City of the Legions, Caerleon-on-Usk. But even this finds no warrant in the British traditions. The Welsh Triads, our most ancient source for Arthur's court, place it at Celliwic in Cornwall – Callington, or more probably, Killibury Castle.[7] Even this attribution is far removed from Arthur's own day, and those documents which are contemporary with Arthur himself are completely silent concerning the whereabouts of his court, even about its existence.

Where, then, does the idea of Camelot come from? The name first appears in the variant manuscripts of the romance *Lancelot*, composed by the French poet Chrétien de Troyes in the late twelfth century. What had happened was that Chrétien and his successors, with characteristic medieval anachronism, saw Arthur as a medieval monarch. They then had to provide him with a court, a castle, a principal centre; and, lacking any authentic traditions, they invented Camelot. Perhaps the name itself was shortened from the British and Roman *Camulodunum* (Colchester). This, in the form *Camalodunum Britanniae oppidum*, has a passing reference in the Elder Pliny's *Natural History*, a work which was certainly much read in western Europe in the twelfth century. But wherever they found the name, the French poets were inconsistent about its spelling – Camalot, Caamalot, and Camahaloth are among the variants which occur – and they are, of course, completely vague about its location.[8]

This topographical vagueness inevitably persisted when the idea of Camelot was introduced to England. It is mentioned once only in the fourteenth-century poem, *Sir Gawain and the Green Knight*, and there is not the least indication where the anonymous poet thought it might be. In fact, the first suggestion of a down-to-earth location comes in the fifteenth century, in Malory's *Le Morte Darthur*, where it is regularly identified with Winchester. It is possible that this attribution was influenced by the purported 'Round Table', a relic of some medieval tourney, which hung then, as it still does, in the hall of Winchester castle. But Malory's identification was not invariably accepted. Even his own editor and printer, Caxton, in the preface to the first published version of *Le Morte Darthur*, silently rejected it. Instead, he referred to the evidence for Arthur 'in Wales, in the toune of Camelot, which dyvers now lyvyng hath seen'.[9] Was Caxton, under the influence of Geoffrey of Monmouth, thinking of Caerleon; or was he referring to the Roman walls of Caerwent, still upstanding even today? Whatever his reasons, Caxton had thrown open the whole question of the location of Camelot, and thereby made it possible for Leland to suggest yet a third identification: Cadbury Castle. And from Leland's day on, a great body of literary, topographical and antiquarian tradition has maintained that identification down to the Ordnance Survey's plans of the area.

Fig. 3

The historical reality of Arthur himself is in no way linked to that of Camelot, and to impugn the authenticity of the one is not to cast doubt on the other. It needs no saying that over the centuries fabulous tales and romances have become attached to Arthur's name. This process had certainly begun by the ninth century, if not by the late sixth.[10] Nevertheless, these fictions do not of themselves discredit the figure to whom they are attached, for it is a commonplace that even in modern times apochryphal tales may be told about great men within their own lifetimes. The significance of the Arthurian romances for our purpose is that they present the historian with a very complex problem of analysis. He has to determine which events in the story of Arthur were recorded within living memory, for these are likely to be historical.

It would be out of place to recapitulate all the arguments involved here, and it is enough to state quite baldly the conclusions arrived at in the latest analysis of the sources.[11] Two facts about Arthur were noted down in the

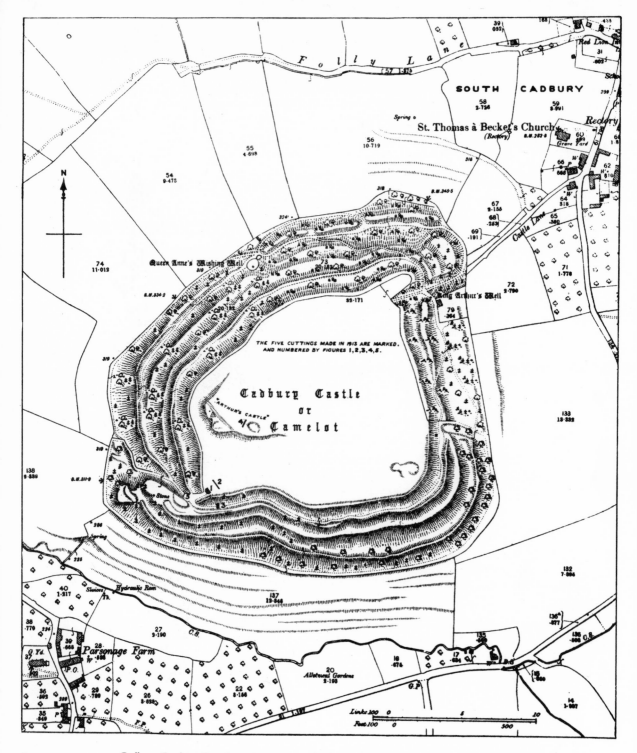

3 *Cadbury Castle or Camelot as it appears on the Ordnance Survey plans. The 1913 excavations are marked 1–5. The Roman site explored in South Cadbury village lies immediately south of St Thomas à Becket's church*

records maintained in some British monastery, in the year in which they actually occurred. First, he took part in the Battle of Badon 'and the Britons were victors'; and second, Arthur and Medraut, or Modred, perished in the battle of Camlann. Unfortunately we do not possess the original document in which these events were recorded, only a twelfth-century copy of a tenth-century abstract of it or of some intervening copy. In the process of copying or abstracting, the year-by-year dates which would have been a feature of the original record have been lost, and so we are left with a series of annals running from Year 1 to Year 533. To some extent we can calibrate the annals by placing against important events such dates as we can obtain from other historical sources. On this basis, we can calculate that Badon was fought in AD 518, and Camlann in AD 539. It is possible, however, that the chronology here has become confused in the process of copying from one document to another. If this is so, the true date of Badon may be AD 490 or 499. These earlier dates would agree with the belief that Arthur was the successor of the romanized general Ambrosius Aurelianus, who is tied by good historical evidence to the middle decades of the fifth century.

These two references are unimpeachable in terms of the normal rules of historical criticism, and to reject them is to display prejudice, not scholarship. It is impossible to establish any other early source with equal confidence. A ninth-century compilation, the *Historia Brittonum*, contains a Latin abstract of an early Welsh poem which celebrated Arthur's battles. From what we know of such poems, the original may have been composed in Arthur's own day and declaimed in his presence. In that case it would have all the merits of an early source. It is perhaps less likely that it was an elegy composed after his death, displaying a romantic rather than an historical image. Whatever the truth may be, no convincing identifications have ever been proposed for the actual sites of the battles listed in the *Historia Brittonum*, or for Badon and Camlann, though it is generally accepted that Badon was fought against Saxon invaders somewhere in southern England.

Returning to the two early records, they do at least assure us that Arthur was a genuine person, and a great one at that, or else he would not have been mentioned at all. He appears as a soldier, not as a king, and two phrases in the *Historia Brittonum* imply that he was leader of some kind of combined force on behalf of several British kingdoms. What little we can discern about the history of Britain in the fifth and sixth centuries shows that after Roman rule had been shaken off about 410, the Roman diocese of Britain split apart into a number of small kingdoms ruled by *tyranni* or usurpers. Some degree of unity was preserved, however, by an overlord or high king who could initiate military action on behalf of Britain as a whole. For instance, the sixth-century monk Gildas tells us that a certain high king (whom he does not name) employed Saxon mercenaries to defend Britain against the Picts. Through the obscurities of Gildas's Latin we can discern Ambrosius as the general commanding a combined British force, and probably responsible to this same king or his successor. In the decades around 500, Arthur took over Ambrosius's role, with great, but temporary, success. In the long run, the internecine strife of Camlann revealed the political divisions of the British kingdoms, and put an end to any united resistance to the Anglo-Saxon settlers.

Our earliest sources, as we have seen, do not allow us to localize Arthur's military activity. Indeed, they rather suggest that it was extensive, for the battle of Mount Badon was almost certainly fought in southern England, whereas Cat Coit Celidon, the 'battle of the Caledonian Forest', which is mentioned in the *Historia Brittonum*, was in Scotland, more probably in the Southern Uplands than in the Highlands. If Arthur's battles really were so widespread, this may owe something to his political position as agent of a number of kingdoms, but it owes more to the mobility of his forces. Early Welsh poetry shows that they would have ridden to battle, and would then have fought sometimes from horseback in a series of uncoordinated rushes, and sometimes dismounted. In any case, we cannot pin Arthur down to any one region or place. None of the Arthur place-names – Arthur's Seat, the various Arthur's Stones, the Round Tables, and so on – has any valid connection with him, and some refer to archaeological monuments separated from his day by two or three thousand years.

Nevertheless, it seems reasonable to think that the historical Arthur might have had a principal stronghold or military base for his combined force, and no less reasonable to hope that such a base might be identified in archaeological terms. But because of the silence of our earliest historical sources, we know neither its location nor its original name. In the circumstances, it seems legitimate to use 'Camelot' as the name of this hypothetical Arthurian stronghold. What we are doing here is in effect to turn a poetic symbol into an historical one.

At this point, the initiative in research passes from the historian to the archaeologist, who must determine whether or not there is anything in the archaeological record which might correspond with this symbolic Camelot, and might turn it into a reality. In the 1950s, newly-won archaeological evidence suggested that Cadbury Castle could have been such an Arthurian base or stronghold, so to Cadbury we now return.

From antiquarianism to archaeology at Cadbury Castle

Whatever Arthurian associations Cadbury had in Leland's day, in the following centuries it certainly acquired the full repertory of Arthurian folk-lore – the sleeping king in the hollow hill, the ghostly ride, and so on. Here we are concerned not with these things, so much as with the historical facts about Arthur and the archaeological facts about Cadbury. What is certain is that the Arthurian connection continued to attract the attention of antiquarian and topographic writers, who recorded, either at first hand or by simple repetition from their predecessors, the discovery of ancient buildings and ancient relics upon the hill. One of the best accounts is that by William Stukeley, who visited 'Camalet Castle' in 1723, and this must stand here as representative of three centuries of observation and speculation.[12]

'Camalet is a noted place', he wrote. 'It is a noble fortification of the Romans, placed on the north end of a ridge of hills separated from the rest by nature; and for the most part solid rock, very steep and high: there are three or four ditches quite round, sometimes more: the *area* within is twenty acres at least, rising in the middle: its figure is squarish, but conforms to the shape of the hill. There is a higher angle of ground within, ditched about, where they say was king Arthur's palace: it was probably the *praetorium*, and might be king Arthur's too, who lived in this place: the country people refer all stories to him. The whole has been ploughed over since the memory of man, and much stone has been taken from the surface, which has altered it. The rampart is large and high, made chiefly of great stones covered with earth, and perhaps, in some parts where it was necessary, laid with mortar. In this camp they find many pebble-stones exactly round, half a peck at a time; whereas there are none such in the country: they suppose them stones to sling withal, fetched from the sea, or perhaps shot in cross-bows. Roman coin in great plenty has been found here: I saw vast numbers of Antoninus and Faustina. They have dug up square stones, door-jambs with hinges, and say there are subterraneous vaults thereabouts. Selden, in his notes on *Polyolbion*, writes it was full of ruins and reliques of old buildings. At top they told me many pavements and arches have been dug up, hand-grind-stones, and other domestic or camp utensils.' Most of this seems the result of close and sound observation, though we might doubt whether 'pavements and arches' had ever been dug up; it is more likely that the natural slabby limestone of the top of the hill had been mistaken for artificial pavements.

Stukeley's account seems to have been based entirely on relics and remains turned up in the course of ploughing and of quarrying for stone. For the beginnings of purposeful excavation, we have to wait until the late nineteenth century, when the Rev. James A. Bennett, Rector of South Cadbury and Secretary of the Somersetshire Archaeological and Natural History Society began delving into the hill as well as collecting traditions about it.[13] Bennett is our best source for the mature development of folk-lore about Cadbury, with his tales of corn stacks sinking into the hollow hill, and of querns used by fairies on the hill-top, but regrettably he left no systematic account of his diggings. He mentions 'opening up a hut dwelling upon the plain of the hill', in which he found potsherds, and half a large quern. His 'hut dwelling' was most probably an Iron Age storage pit, for these used to be interpreted as 'pit-dwellings'.

Bennett also cut a trench thirteen feet deep through the innermost rampart, observed the different layers which were present, and recorded that 'as we went down the pottery decreased in quantity and increased in coarseness'. From this he very sensibly concluded that 'there must have been a considerable interval between the beginning and the completion of the rampart, and that a rude race who began it had to give way to another in a higher state of civilization, and this it would seem, from the differences in the remains at different levels, may have happened more than once'. Eighty years on, after considerable exploration of the ramparts, we can only expand on the text originally preached by Bennett.

Bennett himself had little idea of the age of the pottery and other objects which he found. He recognized the Roman coins, of course, and even 'a British coin, earlier than the Romano-British coinage'. Beyond this he could only speculate that his finds probably belonged 'to different dates, some ante-Roman, some Roman or post-Roman'. It was left to H. St George Gray, the father-figure of Somerset archaeology, to analyse the relics found by Bennett, noting that most of them 'may be referred to the Late-Celtic Period (dating approximately from 200 BC to AD 100)'; noting too the occurrence of flint implements of Neolithic type, but rejecting altogether the suggestion that 'the camp was constructed and occupied in the Stone Age'.[14]

Fig. 3

The occasion of St George Gray's comments was a report on his own trial-excavation, carried out with six labourers from 17 June to 24 June 1913. This was a mere scratching at the surface of the great hillfort, but it has considerable historical importance for a number of reasons. Firstly, Gray himself bridges the gap between nineteenth- and twentieth-century archaeology in Britain. Consistent with his early training as assistant to the pioneer archaeologist Pitt Rivers, he recorded the location of his trenches, and the exact positions of the principal finds, in a way which would have been unthinkable to Bennett. But, most important, Gray's major excavations at the Glastonbury and Meare Lake Villages are the principal foundation for our knowledge of the Iron Age culture of south-western England. His conclusions that the relics from Cadbury belonged principally 'to the Late-Celtic Period', and that 'Camelot has produced conclusive evidence of Late-Celtic and Roman occupation' established for a generation that our site was a perfectly normal hillfort, built in the Iron Age, and re-used in some fashion in the Roman period as well. There was little room here for speculation about Camelot and Arthur.

Fig. 2

Camelot revived

The possibility that Cadbury Castle had a connection with Arthur and with Camelot was revived in the mid-1950s, as a result partly of chance discovery, partly of systematic research. At this time, the interior of the Cadbury defences, which had been in pasture for a period, was cultivated for several years. As in the days of Leland and Stukeley, coins and other relics were turned up by the plough; and, as in earlier centuries, most of these relics disappeared, unrecorded, into private collections. All the more credit is due therefore to one amateur collector, the late Mrs Mary Harfield, who not only picked up pottery, flints, and other objects on a systematic basis, but also noted where her finds had come from and, even more important, presented them to a public institution, the Somerset County Museum at Taunton. Mrs Harfield's material, together with objects collected by J. Stevens Cox, were examined by Ralegh Radford, the leading figure in Dark-Age studies in western Britain. He recognized among them pottery of Early Neolithic date, as well as Iron Age material considerably older than the Late-Celtic pottery distinguished by Gray. These discoveries must be deferred until Chapter II. For our present purpose, what matters was Dr Radford's recognition that some pottery could be dated to the late fifth and sixth centuries – the period in which the historical Arthur had been active.

It was entirely due to Dr Radford's own researches that such pottery was distinguishable. In the 1930s, in the course of excavating an early Celtic monastery which underlay the medieval castle of Tintagel in Cornwall, he had found pottery which was without known parallels in Britain, but for which a southern Gaulish origin and a Dark-Age date seemed possible. Subsequent research on existing collections, together with new material from other excavations, made it possible in the mid-1950s to present a systematic account of what could now be called the 'imported pottery found at Tintagel, Cornwall: an aspect of British trade with the Mediterranean in the Early Christian period'.[15] Dr Radford showed that similar pottery was common in the East Mediterranean, including Athens, Constantinople, and Egypt, and that a date in the fifth and sixth centuries was most probable.

Plate XIII

The seminal paper on the Tintagel pottery contained, in a postscript, a note of some five lines on the comparable pottery found by Mrs Harfield at South Cadbury. A fuller account, by Ralegh Radford and Stevens Cox, appeared about the same time in the *Proceedings* of the Somerset Archaeological Society. After describing and illustrating characteristic fragments of

Figs. 27, 28

pottery and a piece of Dark-Age glass, the authors concluded: 'the small collection indicates an occupation during the fifth, sixth, or early seventh century and provides an interesting confirmation of the traditional identification of the site as the Camelot of Arthurian legend'.[16]

With hindsight, and recalling what I have already said about the fabulous character of Camelot, it is possible to see that this statement was rather questionable in historical terms. At the time, however, it did not appear this way. The new evidence made it possible to assert that Cadbury was a military site in use at the time when Arthur was a warrior. So these new archaeological discoveries, when compared with those of Bennett and St George Gray, put quite a different complexion on the traditional Arthurian associations of Cadbury. And this in turn created a new interest in the site, in both professional and amateur circles, which eventually bore fruit in the summer of 1965, in the formation of the Camelot Research Committee.

The founding Chairman of the Committee was, naturally, Dr Radford. The onerous and unrewarding task of Secretary was filled by Geoffrey Ashe, writer of distinguished middle-brow books on the problems of the historical Arthur. Shortly after its formation, the committee was strengthened by Sir Mortimer Wheeler's acceptance of the Presidency. The committee itself represented a very wide spectrum of Arthurian – and even non-Arthurian – interests, from the most austere learned societies through to amateur bodies who had only a boundless enthusiasm to contribute. Its principal term of reference was to promote a large-scale excavation of Cadbury Castle, and its first task was to raise funds adequate to that purpose. After several flirtations with professional fund-raisers, it became apparent that the more conventional type of appeal for funds was likely to be altogether more rewarding. But first it was necessary to know whether or not the site justified a large project and a commensurate appeal. The committee therefore charged me, in the summer of 1966, with the direction of a reconnaissance investigation, in order to examine both the feasibility and the desirability of large-scale research.

Before that reconnaissance is described in Chapter II, it seems opportune to clarify certain matters about the Camelot Research Committee and its policy. For a start, it may be said that the ideas held by individual members of the committee about Arthur and Camelot ranged from an uncritical belief in the most romantic and unhistorical tales, through a vague but uninformed scepticism which might be combined with a very lively interest in the archaeology of the fifth and sixth centuries, to a degree of scholarship unrivalled in the Arthurian field.

My own position, when I was invited to serve as the committee's Director of Excavations, was that I had no first-hand knowledge of the historical issues involved. I was prepared to accept the historical reality of Arthur and the authenticity of Camelot as working hypotheses. In the event, my own historical researches during the course of the excavation brought me to the position outlined above: the affirmation of Arthur and the rejection of Camelot. From the archaeological, as opposed to the historical point of view, however, I had worked intensively on fortified sites in Arthurian Britain, and on their economic and social background. I was particularly interested in Cadbury because it did not fit my general picture of the fortifications of the period. Indeed, its very existence was a challenge to my ideas, and stimulated a desire to investigate it thoroughly.

But the interest of Cadbury Castle extended beyond its Arthurian occupation. The evidence for settlement in the Iron Age has already been mentioned, and Neolithic activity has been hinted at. Moreover, in the late 1950s it had been shown conclusively that, under the Old English name *Cadanbyrig*, Cadbury had held an emergency mint of King Ethelred the Unready (978–1016). In other words, even before the excavations began, it appeared that the site had witnessed an unusually long span of human activity, which marked it off from the general run of southern English hillforts. If the results of our reconnaissance confirmed this appearance, then Cadbury would merit excavation on the largest scale. And if that proved possible, it was the firm purpose both of the committee and of myself as Director of Excavations that the whole history of the hill-top should receive attention consistent with the actual archaeological remains.

Fig. 34

This, then, was the spirit in which the committee laid its plans, and in which the reconnaissance of 1966 was organized. To that investigation, and the subsequent geophysical prospecting, we now turn.

II   Reconnaissance 1966–1967

The topographical data

Before the 1966 plan of campaign can be described, it is necessary to set out the data on which that campaign was based: in other words, the topographical, archaeological and historical information that was already available before the Camelot Research Committee's excavations began. The Arthurian data have already been described in sufficient detail, and here attention will be concentrated firstly on the general aspect of the hill, and secondly on other periods in the history of the site.

Plate 1

Figs. 3, 4

Cadbury Castle occupies a free-standing hill towards the eastern border of Somerset. The summit is a little over five hundred feet above Ordnance Datum, with the hill itself standing about two hundred and fifty feet above the surrounding countryside. Geologically-speaking, it consists of bands of a hard Oolitic limestone and of a softer yellow sandstone characteristic of the Yeovil Beds. The disposition of these bands suggests a major fault line running roughly west-north-west to east-south-east. In the scarp formed by the fault there are soft pockets and even minor chasms in the rock which lend themselves to romantic speculations about hollow hills and sleeping kings. There is no water on the hill-top itself, but at the north-east corner, about one hundred feet below the summit, a natural spring has been built over to make 'King Arthur's Well'.

To the east, at a distance of under a mile, the view is blocked by hills a hundred feet or so higher, which mark the western scarp of the higher ground of Wessex. Interrupted only slightly by the valley of the Stour, this high ground runs through to Salisbury Plain. To the south are the more distant hills of north Dorset and south Somerset, with the great fortress of Ham Hill darkly visible. But west and north the whole Somerset basin opens up, with a view which on a clear day extends to the islands of the Bristol Channel, and even the hills of Glamorgan. The principal feature of this extensive plain is the conical hill of Glastonbury Tor, eleven miles north-west of Cadbury. This immediately evokes thoughts of Arthur's burial at Glastonbury – which may have more substance than historians have recently allowed[17] – and of the rich and famous Iron Age 'lake-villages' of Glastonbury and Meare.

Before the visitor can enjoy these views, he must first pass through the defences either from South Cadbury, by means of the north-east gate, or from Sutton Montis by the south-west gate. The defences themselves are sited where the original hill-slope was steepest. The innermost is between twenty and sixty feet vertically below the summit, and from it three or even four banks range down the slope over a vertical distance of almost one hundred and fifty feet, more than half the total height of the hill. The two principal entrance passages rise steeply through the banks, but in the case of the South Cadbury gate the apparent steepness is partly the result of erosion. The right-hand side of each entrance is overshadowed by a projection of the ramparts, which is probably based on a natural spur of the hill. On the eastern side there is a third entrance, which is also ancient, but nothing is known of its history. On this side, moreover, the two outer banks have been obliterated, probably in the course of farming over the last few centuries.

Within the defences is an area of about eighteen acres, which is far from uniform in its aspect. Roughly one quarter of the hill-top, lying above four hundred and ninety feet O.D., forms a broad summit ridge or plateau, which slopes gently from west-north-west to east-south-east. On the west and south-west the plateau is edged by a steep scarp, which is partly but not entirely the result of quarrying. Elsewhere the plateau dips off into slopes which are more moderate but still steepish. Towards the rear of the rampart these slopes level off in a zone fifty feet or more in width, which is clearly the result of soil loosened by the plough coming to rest against the back of the inner bank. These three distinct areas – the level zone, the slopes, and the plateau – all merited separate attention during the reconnaissance.

Plates 26, I, VII

The archaeological and historical data

The archaeological data came partly from the objects deposited in Taunton Museum by Bennett and others; partly from St George Gray's limited scratchings in 1913; and principally from the material collected by Mrs Harfield, Stevens Cox, and others in the 1950s. These collections, for a start, put the Neolithic activity at Cadbury in quite a different light from that in which it had appeared to Gray. He knew only of axes and other flint implements, which might have been lost in the course of forest clearance or hunting, and he could therefore reject the idea that the hill had been occupied

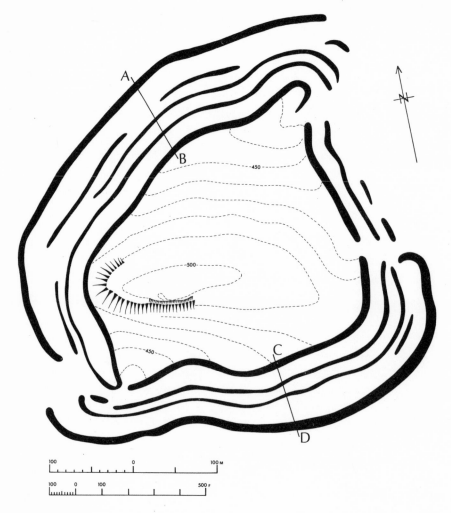

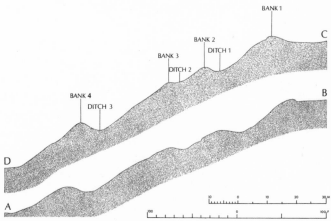

4 Simplified plan of the defences of Cadburý Castle, with profiles across them

in the Stone Age. Now, however, the discovery of a fair quantity of characteristic Neolithic pottery made it far more likely that there had been a permanent settlement on the hill-top. But there was nothing to show what kind of settlement it might have been.

The Bronze Age remained a blank in the Cadbury record, but the Iron Age now appeared to extend well back behind the 'Late-Celtic Period (200 BC to AD 100)' diagnosed by St George Gray. In particular, the publication of distinctive coarse jars with finger-tip ornament on the shoulder and the rim suggested that Cadbury had been inhabited in the fifth or fourth centuries BC, as early as any Iron Age hillfort known at that time in southern Britain. This in turn implied the probability – as Bennett had already suggested – of a long and complex history in the defences.

Another piece of information, which extended the history of the site in the other direction, came from the researches of numismatists, principally Mr Michael Dolley. Silver pennies of Ethelred the Unready with a mint-mark CADANBYRIG or CADANBYRIM have, indeed, long been known. Many examples have been found in Scandinavia, because Ethelred paid tens of thousands of pounds to the Vikings in an attempt to buy them off. It had been surmised that the Cadanbyrig in question was our Cadbury, but the name was too common in south-west England for the identification to be certain. The coins, however, bear not only the name of Ethelred and the place of minting, but also the names of the individual moneyers who struck them. Dolley was able to show that late in Ethelred's reign certain moneyers were moved from Ilchester to Cadanbyrig; and that early in the succeeding reign of Cnut, they were moved from Cadanbyrig, either back to Ilchester or on to Crewkerne or Bruton. South Cadbury fits this triangular movement so exactly that the identification was clinched. The further probabilities were that the coin-mint would have been inside a *burh* or fortified town and that the *burh* would have been on top of the Cadbury hill and would have re-used the Iron Age defences. Our excavations therefore promised a priceless opportunity of investigating a Late Saxon town which had not been built over in medieval and modern times.

Fig. 34

One further set of data was available to us. In 1955 the hill-top had been sown with oats, and in June of that year Mrs Harfield noticed dark patches in the ripening crop. Such patches, known to the archaeologist as 'crop-marks', indicate pits and ditches dug into the solid rock. During the summer months, these pits retain more moisture than the surrounding soil, and the crop above them ripens more slowly; in other words, it remains green longer. Crop-marks are best seen and recorded from the air, so with great enterprise Mrs Harfield arranged for Cadbury to be photographed by the Royal Naval Air Station at Yeovilton.[18] At about the same time, another local amateur, Mr M. C. Jones, was able to use his position with Westland Aircraft at Yeovil to photograph the crop-marks. These air-photos should have been of great assistance in planning the excavations, but both sets suffered from various snags. All were of low contrast, so that the crop-marks did not appear at all strongly. The negatives of the RNAS photos had been lost, so that it was not possible to manipulate the prints. And all the view-points were oblique, not vertical, so that it was difficult to pinpoint on the ground any features which seemed of particular interest on the photos.

At this point, the layman might wonder why we did not simply ask the RNAS to re-photograph the hill, or employ some commercial air-photo-grapher to do this, so that we had photos which met our needs. The answer is that the marks show only in ripening cereal-crops, not in pasture – and we could scarcely ask the landowners to sow the site with oats so that we could then photograph crop-marks! As it was, Mr Jones displayed very great ingenuity in trying to correct the distortion caused by the obliquity of the viewpoint, and did succeed in producing some near-vertical prints on which major features could be located. But in general, the principal importance of the air-photos was to demonstrate that the whole hill-top had been intensively occupied – if, that is, the black dots which marked ancient refuse pits were a valid index of occupation.

Resources and organization

My original intention in 1966 had been to restrict our reconnaissance to a detailed survey of Cadbury, both of the defences and of the area inside them. The reason for this was simple. When I was appointed Director of Excava-tions, my knowledge of the fort was limited to a brief visit in the company of other people. If I was to plan large-scale excavations at all effectively, I needed to know the site in great detail – to get the subjective feel of it as well as to learn its objective shape and pattern. And the best way to do this was to spend three weeks making a comprehensive survey.

I was persuaded, however, that it would also be useful to test the archaeo-logical layers inside the fort, if only because there was good reason to fear that they had been largely destroyed by ploughing. Indeed, reading the antiquaries' accounts of the coins, pottery, sling-stones and so on that had been dug up over the last four centuries, it seemed doubtful whether there would be either layers or relics left for a modern archaeologist to find. So I agreed to take a small digging team along with the surveyors. Somehow this snowballed into a labour-force which was quite sizable by normal standards: about fifty staff and volunteer workers for a period of just over three weeks.

The principal resources for the reconnaissance, in the three equally necessary components of brains, brawn and cash, came from University College, Cardiff. Here it is appropriate to pay a special tribute to the five generations of Cardiff students, both graduate and under-graduate, who effectively ran the Cadbury dig. It is true that over five years the excavation attracted a few competent supervisors from outside, and that we also trained up several outstanding workers who came to us from elsewhere; but the overwhelming majority of our supervisory staff were from the Cardiff Department of Archaeology. The sheer size of the excavation in the four main seasons meant that very little control could be exercised in detail by the Director; and the success of the work was therefore principally due to the skill and devotion of the site supervisors and their assistants.

In addition to the financial backing of University College, Cardiff, funds were provided by learned societies, notably the British Academy and the Society of Antiquaries of London; and also by the Bristol United Press and the British Broadcasting Corporation. These last two grants were symptomatic of the great, and on the whole helpful, interest taken in the project by the Press and broadcasting media. But over the years the largest single item in our budget came from private donations, and especially from the offerings made on the site by the hordes of visitors who had been shown something of the excavation and the finds. Our conducted tours and exhibition of finds were, indeed, a special feature of the Cadbury excavations. In part our motive was the disinterested one of educating the sightseers who throng to any archaeological dig, but the financial returns formed a very important part of our income.

A major point of fund-raising policy was involved here. In 1966, we found that a firm of fund-raisers was prepared to carry out a pilot survey to examine the feasibility of raising the £15,000 or so which we needed for large-scale excavations. For the pilot survey, they would charge £700. At the end of it, they might report unfavourably, in which case the money would have been thrown away; even if they had thought it possible to raise funds, most of the work would have to be done by the committee by means of jumble-sales, coffee-mornings, and simple begging. It was obviously better to use our limited funds – which did not even amount to £700 – on an archaeological pilot survey, with two objectives: first, to demonstrate the

29

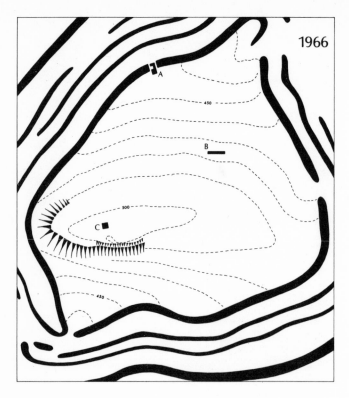

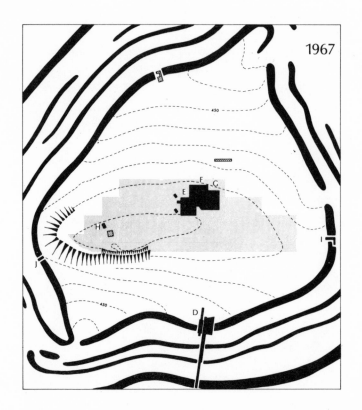

5 *The progress of excavation (solid black) and of geophysical survey (stippled), 1966–69. (For the 1970 season, see Fig. 9)*

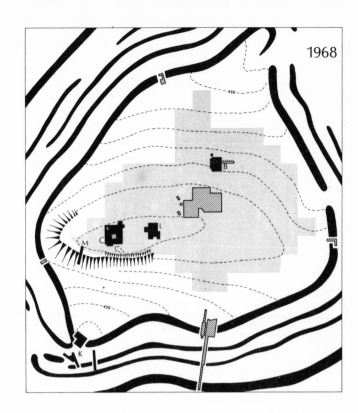

1968

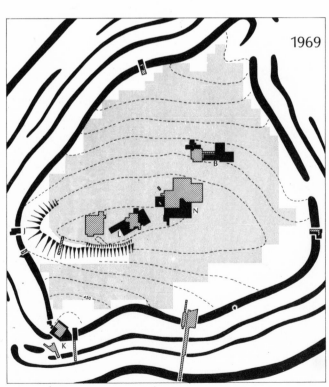

1969

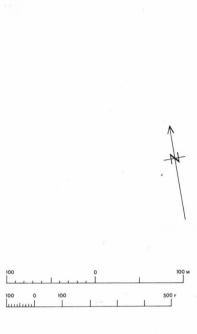

31

importance of Cadbury in terms of archaeological scholarship to the learned societies which must always provide the basic funds for major research programmes; and secondly to awaken a widespread and popular interest in a site which had so much to offer, both scenically and historically, to the ordinary man and his family on holiday, in the hope that this would yield returns in private donations. With this in mind, publicity was deliberately sought, the Press and broadcasting media were given every encouragement, and in 1966 I seemed to spend more time as a public relations officer than as an archaeological director. Since this gave my staff the chance to get on with survey and digging free from directorial interference, no harm was done.

As a fund-raising programme, this was manifestly successful. On two occasions – in the spring of 1968, and at the end of 1969 – the Committee was momentarily disturbed by the lack of balance between the Director's proposed expenditure and the actual money in hand, but in each case the deficit was made good. Over the five seasons, plans formulated to meet the needs of research were never curtailed by lack of cash.

Survey and excavation, 1966

Fig. 3

Fig. 4

Since an acceptable working plan of the Cadbury defences was already in existence in the form of the large-scale Ordnance Survey plans, our own survey could concentrate on more refined details. It was necessary to study the defences thoroughly as a preliminary to excavating them, and the best way to examine them was to survey profiles across them on all sides of the hill. This exercise was more akin to jungle warfare than to normal archaeological surveying. So heavy is the tree-cover and undergrowth around most of the perimeter that it was necessary to begin each profile by hacking lines of sight through the jungle. Beneath the trees, the ramparts appeared as bare earth at a high angle, and in wet weather the lines of sight became mud slides, on which the surveyors slithered about for hours on end. Despite their difficulties, the result was an informative series of profiles, and an enhanced impression of the formidable character of Cadbury's defences.

In the interior, our principal aim was to delimit the areas most convenient for building – the places where human occupation was most likely to be concentrated, and the most rewarding, therefore, for the excavator. A very detailed contour plan seemed the best way to achieve this. It was already obvious that the summit plateau was the most suitable for buildings because of its flatness, while the south-western scarp was impossibly steep. These two

1 Before the excavations. Cadbury Castle and South Cadbury village seen from
the air in 1966. This view, looking almost due west, shows how the Cadbury hill
and its defences stand up above the Somerset lowlands. The Romano-British
settlement excavated in South Cadbury by Mr John Laidlaw (pp. 51, 170, 172) lies
between the church and the cottages to its left. From the cottages a track slopes up
to the left towards the north-east entrance of Cadbury Castle, which is concealed
by the heavy growth of trees. The inner rampart is visible around most of the hill-
top, and Banks 2 and 3 can be seen at the south-east corner. Below the tree-line are
the agricultural terraces known as 'The Linches' (p. 203)

2 William Stukeley's drawing of the ramparts of Cadbury Castle as they appeared from the north in 1723 (p. 11). The apparent number of ramparts is exaggerated because the drawing does not distinguish between defensive works and agricultural terraces; but the steepness of the ramparts is faithfully depicted

3 The model of Cadbury Castle made by the BBC to show the defences as they would have appeared before trees were planted on them. A simple palisade has been reconstructed on top of the inner bank (p.11)

4, 5 RNAS air-photographs showing the crop-marks visible in the summer of 1955 (pp. 27–8). The top view is looking south-east, the lower one looking west. The two hollow-ways leading up from the north-east entrance to the summit ridge are visible as broad black marks in a rough V formation (pp. 50, 74). The well-defined black blobs indicate rock-cut pits for storage or refuse (pp. 73, 136)

6, 7 The pulsed magnetic induction locator and the soil anomaly detector ('banjo') being used by teams from Oxford and Cardiff (pp. 52–5)

8 Excavation on the summit plateau in 1967. The topsoil has been removed from Site F, and rock-cut pits and ditches, closely corresponding with geophysical anomalies, are beginning to appear (p. 70)

9 Site EFG at the end of the 1967 season. The principal features are: the cruciform trench (*Fig. 10, 29*) bottom left; the field boundary (*Fig. 10, 3*); and the Iron Age ring-ditch (*Fig. 10, 21*). For a plan of the area, see *Fig. 8*

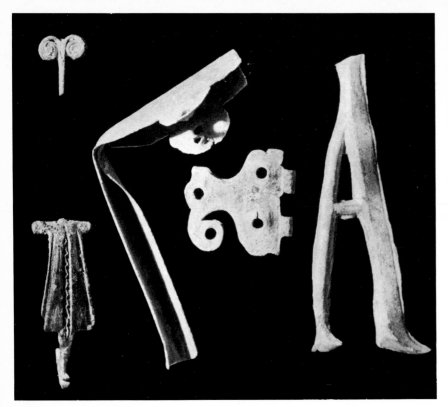

10 Bronze objects found in 1966. Late Bronze Age spiral-headed pin (p. 50); Iron Age fiddle brooch (*Fig. 26*); Roman shield-binding and cuirass hinge (p. 51 and Plates 70–2); gilt-bronze letter, perhaps from an inscription at a Romano-Celtic temple (p. 51). Actual size

11 Significant finds in 1967. Neolithic flint arrowhead (p. 108); Late Bronze Age socketed knife (p. 114); Early Iron Age swan's neck pin (p. 122); Celtic bronze brooches, the pins missing (p. 168); Iron Age scabbard chape of bronze; gilt-bronze Saxon button brooch (see Plate XIV); two Celtic coins (pp. 166–7); Roman coin of the Emperor Claudius (p. 160). The knife is 3 ins long

12, 13 Air-view and key-plan of Sites P, S, and T at the end of the 1970 season. 1 – 4 probable rectangular buildings (see *Fig. 11*); 5 – 8 wall-slots of round houses; 9 fence bounding area of animal-burials; 10 shrine (pp. 163–4); 11 medieval or later field boundary; 12 rectangular building, possibly ancillary to the sixth-century hall; 13 site of hall (*Fig. 30*); 14 furnace area (p. 156). Note also the large administrative tail to the excavations: finds hut, pottery-washing area, director's and supervisors' huts, and marquee for workers

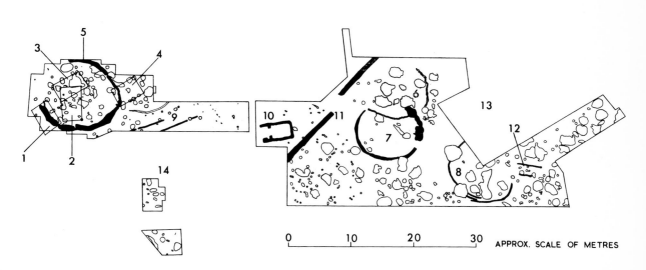

APPROX. SCALE OF METRES

14 Excavation of the southern defences in 1967. Cutting D across Banks 2, 3 and 4, and Ditches 1, 2, and 3. Section-drawing is in progress in Ditch 1. This was the only line across the defences which was completely clear of trees

15 The excavation of the
defences in 1967, seen from
the bottom of Ditch 3. The
nearest figure is working
on the scarp of Ditch 3; the
third figure up the trench
stands on bedrock beneath
Bank 3; the fourth figure
in the trench is on the crest
of Bank 2; and the skyline
is formed by Bank 1. This
view is greatly fore-
shortened, and gives no
adequate impression of the
steepness of the slope; but
this may be judged from
the need to cut sloping
pathways (right of trench)
and to provide a safety line
(left of trench). See Plate 28
for the view down the
trench, and *Fig. 21* for the
profile of the ditches

16, 17 Air-photographs of the excavations in 1969. The upper view is looking north, the lower one south-west. Work is in progress on Sites K, L, N, and B. See *Fig.* 5

18–20 Excavation of the Neolithic pit P154. At the top is a human skeleton, badly mutilated by ploughing, which overlay the pit. The date of the skeleton is not yet established, but it may not be Neolithic, and its association with the pit may be coincidental. *Centre* and *bottom*, the contents of the pit, including a human lower jaw; ribs and jaws from ox and pig; fragment of deer antler; flint flakes and Neolithic pottery (p. 110). The pit has given radiocarbon dates of 2510 ± 120 BC and 2825 ± 115 BC (p. 112)

21 A Late Neolithic stake-hole discovered beneath Bank 1 on Site A (pp. 102, 113). Scale of centimetres

22 Late Neolithic pottery in the Rinyo-Clacton style found beside the stake-hole. For a reconstruction drawing, see *Fig. 14*

23 Some significant bronzes. Early Bronze Age flanged axe, 4 ins long (p. 113). Late Bronze Age socketed spear-head (p. 114). Hallstatt razor and swan's neck pin, intrusive elements in the Initial and Early Iron Age (pp. 120, 122)

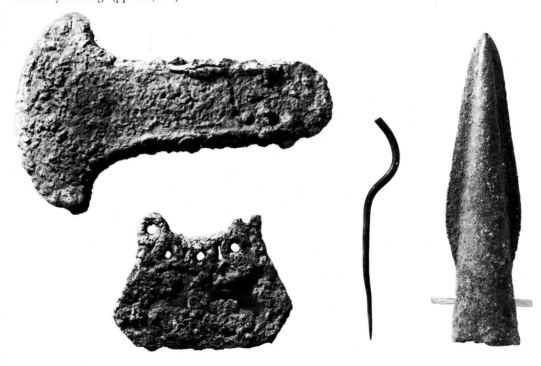

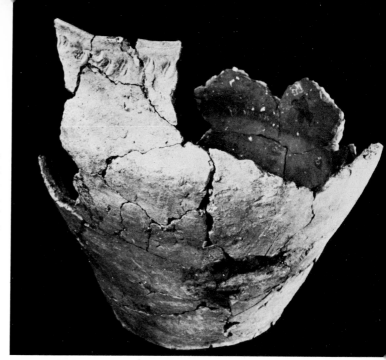

24, 25 Late Bronze Age oven-pit, and the pot which lay in it (p. 116). In the view of the pit, half of the wood ash which filled it has been removed, revealing the base and lower wall of the pot still in position from its last use. Scale of centimetres. Reconstruction of the fragments from the pit showed that while almost all of the lower part of the pot was present, most of the rim and upper body had been lifted out. For a drawing of the pot, see *Fig. 16*

26 Air-view of the defences at the south-east corner. Banks 1, 2, and 3 are clear of trees, but Bank 4 is concealed. Compare Plate VII

27 The rock-cut scarp of Ditch 1 as it was revealed in Cutting D. The rubble of Bank 1 is just visible top right; the stone-fall from the bank fills the ditch bottom left. Compare *Fig. 21*

28 Looking down Cutting D from the crest of Bank 1 in 1967. The view is drastically foreshortened, but the diminishing size of the figures gives some impression of scale. For the view looking up the trench see Plate 15; for another view see Plate II

29 Bank 1: the lias-slab revetment to Rampart B (pp. 68–9, 129–30) as revealed in Cutting D in 1968. One-metre ranging poles stand in the slots where timber uprights have decayed. For a reconstruction see *Fig. 19*

30 Details of the front of Ramparts A and B seen in section (compare *Fig. 7*). In the centre foreground (and running under the later stonework) is the ledge on which the lowest beam of the timber revetment of Rampart A was seated. To the right of this are Neolithic levels; to the left three large stones are post-packing for the uprights of Rampart A. The one-metre rod stands against the stone core of Rampart B, and the thin slabs of the lias revetment of that rampart can be seen far left. For reconstructions based on this evidence see *Figs 18* and *19*

limits were easy to define. Between the extremes, however, lay the slopes of the hill. We thought that these would have been inconveniently steep, but that if they had been built on at all, it would have been necessary to cut level platforms. Over subsequent centuries, these platforms would have been largely obscured by the downward drift of plough-soil but we hoped that an accurate contour survey might still detect faint traces of them. In the event, no platforms were located, but we shall see that this was less significant than we had expected in terms of the actual location of buildings.

Meanwhile, each of the three zones which I have already defined was being sampled in a small excavation. On Site A, the level zone against the back of the rampart was examined in the hope that the washing down of plough-soil might have covered and preserved traces of buildings belonging to the later periods of the site. There was, as expected, a considerable depth of plough-soil – around four feet, in fact. But the latest structural level beneath it was no later than the very end of the Iron Age. This was demonstrated by the occurrence of pottery closely comparable with that from the well-known 'War Cemetery' at Maiden Castle in Dorset, which certainly marked the end of the Iron Age at that site. Below this Ultimate Iron Age level at Cadbury was a series of earlier Iron Age deposits, with traces of structures in the form of rough dry-stone walls, and drainage gullies which had probably surrounded circular houses. The limited resources of our reconnaissance prevented the full exploration of these, but our original objective, to determine the character and depth of the archaeological layers, was fully achieved.

Although Site A had been placed against the back of the innermost rampart, and traces of the rear walling appeared in the north face of the cutting, it had been no part of our original plan to examine the actual defences. This policy was modified at the urging of Sir Mortimer Wheeler, President of the Camelot Research Committee. The surveying of profiles across the defences had already revealed a marked step in the outer slope of the inner bank. In the course of a perambulation of the ramparts, Sir Mortimer suggested that this step might mark the face of a late rampart raised upon the decayed top of an earlier one. If this was so, then Cadbury had been refortified some time long after the Iron Age. Could this be the work of Arthur, or of Ethelred? Cutting A was quickly extended across the top of the bank, and revealed a well-laid mortared stone wall, backed by a bank of earth. The character of the masonry made it certain that this was Late Saxon work, and confirmed the identification of Cadbury with the Cadanbyrig of Ethelred's coins.

Fig. 5

Plates 38, 39

Fig. 4, CD

Plate 86

49

Site B had as its primary purpose the examination of the stratification on the sloping part of the interior, where it was reasonable to expect that archaeological layers had been largely destroyed by ploughing. In deciding where to put the trench, we had half the interior to choose from. We decided that the cutting should fulfil the further purpose of examining one of the most prominent crop-marks noted in 1955 – a large but irregular black streak which appeared on both the RNAS photos and those taken by Mr Jones. Despite the obliquity of the air-photos, it was possible to locate this streak with sufficient exactness to lay a trench across it. It was found that the crop-mark had been caused by a wide but shallow ditch – some fifty feet wide by six feet deep. This was clearly not defensive, but both its date and purpose remained obscure. Either side of the ditch we found that ploughing had failed to destroy ancient floors, hearths, and scatters of pottery. Moreover, the relative steepness of the slope had not deterred the early inhabitants of Cadbury from building hereabouts. This had very disturbing implications for our future programme of excavations, because it meant that traces of buildings might be encountered almost anywhere in the eighteen acres of the interior.

Site C was placed close to the summit of the hill, where the air-photos showed a rash of black blobs suggesting rock-cut pits. As we had expected, the ploughing here had gone right down to the solid rock, so that all ancient floor levels had been destroyed. But once we had removed the plough-soil, we could immediately detect features dug into the rock, because they stood out blackly against the golden-brown of the Jurassic limestone. In our excavation, these rock-cut features included both pits dug for storage and used subsequently for refuse, and also holes that had held the uprights of timber buildings. Stains in the soil showed that some of the posts had been massive – up to seventeen inches across. This in turn implied the existence of very substantial buildings on the plateau. Within the small area of the excavation, no building plans were detectable. We could nevertheless speculate that the posts might have belonged to large circular houses, of the kind already well-known on other Iron Age sites. On the other hand, the discovery of pottery of the imported Tintagel type raised the hope that some of the posts had formed part of a rectangular hall of Arthurian date.

The objects found in 1966 added little to the extensive range already known from Mrs Harfield's collection, but that little was of great interest. There was, for instance, a bronze pin with its head formed out of two spiral coils. Such pins have only rarely been found in Britain, and one of them was associated with a Late Bronze Age spearhead. But similar pins were

Plate 10

widely known in the Mediterranean in the ninth and eight centuries BC. So the Cadbury example hinted at far-flung trade connections, and suggested also that there had been some activity on the site in the centuries immediately before the Iron Age. As it happened, the relationship of the cultures of the Iron Age with those of the preceding Bronze Age has been a matter of controversy, and it was evident that the Cadbury excavations could contribute new information to the debate.

There were hints, too, about the end of the Iron Age. Out of seven datable bronze objects found in 1966, three were fragments of Roman soldiers' equipment – a hinge from a cuirass, a buckle which also probably came from a piece of armour, and a binding strip from the edge of a shield. These evidently marked Roman activity on the hill-top itself, and suggested that the native fortification had been one of those stormed by the Roman general Vespasian in the course of his conquest of southern England. There was, however, very little other early Roman material. We shall see later how the history of events on top of the hill was complemented by that which was being established at its foot by Mr John Laidlaw in an independent excavation. In the later Roman period, however, pottery and coins bore witness to renewed activity on the hill, most probably pilgrimages to a Romano-Celtic temple. The big ditch on Site B yielded a gilt-bronze letter 'A' which caused an unnecessary flutter among the Arthurian romantics, but which in reality came from a temple inscription.

Plates 70–72

For the post-Roman centuries, the haul was very slight. No pottery or other objects could be attributed to the Ethelredan *burh*: indeed, the *burh* bank contained only weathered scraps which were over a thousand years old when it was built. For the Arthurian period we had an iron knife, rather formless at first glance, but so like the knives which I had found on the fifth and sixth-century fort of Dinas Powys that I had no doubt about its date. There were also half-a-dozen fragments from wine jars of the Tintagel type to add to those collected by Mrs Harfield. The most significant thing about them was that the best example came from Site C, from that level area which appeared so suitable for large buildings.

Plate 92

The geophysical reconnaissance: instruments and principles

One other event in 1966, of great importance for the future, owed nothing to our careful planning, though we can reasonably claim credit for its exploitation. Among our visitors there were many who came with helpful ideas and comments, like the woman who had seen the image of King Arthur

on her television set during a programme decrying the Arthurian connections of Tintagel; or the electronics engineer who offered to locate the
iron – or golden – gates into the hill where Arthur lies sleeping. At the very
end of the season, a Mr Mark Howell brought to Cadbury an instrument
which he had devised for locating metal objects. (Contrary to popular
belief, the digging up of iron swords, bronze brooches and gold coins is not
a major objective of the archaeologist: he wants to find such things in
relation to buildings, and in association with more common objects such as
pottery, so that he can create a full picture of life on his site.) As it happened,
we quickly discovered that Mr Howell's instrument was sensitive not only
to metal but also to rock-cut features: certainly to large pits, possibly even
to smaller post-holes. We saw at once that this instrument could meet the
deficiency caused by the lack of vertical air photographs, provided we could
carry out a sufficiently extensive programme of prospecting.

Plate 7

It is easier to describe what the Howell instrument does than to explain
why it does it. It consists of a carrying boom with a radio-transmitter at one
end and a receiver coil at the other.[19] The transmitted signal is picked up by
the coil, and is fed into a meter which displays the signal visually. In practice,
both metal objects and disturbances of the sub-soil may distort the signal,
causing fluctuations in the meter reading. Mark Howell believed that these
fluctuations reflected changes in electrical conductivity, and so the instrument was originally known as a Soil Conductivity Meter. But we found
that changes in local magnetic field were at least a factor, and perhaps a
major one, in distorting the signal. It was possible that the instrument was
detecting a whole range of geophysical anomalies, so it came to be known
as the Soil Anomaly Detector. It was perhaps as well that archaeologists had
already christened it the 'banjo' because of its appearance.

The layman may well ask what electrical conductivity and magnetic
fields have to do with archaeology.[20] The answer is that many human
activities – digging defensive ditches, or drainage gullies, or pits for grain-
storage, or holes for posts – cause a major change in the bedrock. When a
ditch or pit that has been dug into a porous or well-drained subsoil becomes
silted-up, it will normally have a higher moisture content than the subsoil,
and therefore a higher electrical conductivity. The organically-enriched
filling of a refuse pit also has quite different magnetic properties from the
rock in which the pit was dug. A hearth, oven or furnace has a magnetic
field all of its own.

Over the previous score of years, archaeologists with a taste for scientific
gadgetry and geophysicists with a hankering for humanity had been en-

deavouring to locate these man-made geophysical anomalies. Having been associated with some of these experiments, I knew a little not only about the failures which get swept under the carpet, but also about the very great possibilities of geophysical prospecting.

The advantages of the 'banjo' were obvious. It was cheap – about a tenth of the price of other available instruments – so I had no difficulty in persuading my own department to buy one. Most other instruments emit brief pulse-like signals, and therefore take their readings at individual points or stations. The 'banjo', on the other hand, transmits a continuous signal, and can therefore give continuous readings. Since it is highly portable, it is possible to search an area swiftly and extensively until an anomaly is located, and then, by moving around, to define the limits of the anomaly with great precision. It was therefore possible to use it for very detailed and refined prospecting. Its disadvantages, as we learned in practice, were that it was not measuring an absolute magnetic field, only relative changes; and that the signal tended to drift to such an extent that it was often impossible to correlate the readings of two areas as little as ten metres apart.

For our purposes, however, the 'banjo' had two overwhelming advantages. Its circuitry was so simple that it was easy to maintain; and it required neither qualifications in electronics nor a knowledge of geophysics for its successful operation. This emboldened us to think that we, as archaeologists, might carry out a comprehensive geophysical survey ourselves. There was nothing revolutionary in this – the pioneers of geophysical prospecting in archaeology, men like R. J. C. Atkinson, had been archaeologists first and last. But recently the geophysicists had tended to take over in the field, with instruments that were both too complicated and too costly for the archaeologist to use. The necessary two-way communication between archaeology and geophysics had become tenuous, with the geophysicists not fully understanding the requirements of the archaeologists, and the latter not appreciating the limitations – or the possibilities – of the instruments. What we wanted to do was to start by formulating our problems in archaeological terms, asking what man-made features we needed information about; then we would match the instrument to the problems; and finally, we would present the results not in terms of ohms and gammas, magnetic fields and electrical resistivity, but in a manner which immediately visualized the archaeological features.

The basic archaeological problem had been posed by the obliquity of the air-photographs. What we now wanted was to locate the rock-cut features shown by the air-photos in such a way that we could pinpoint individual pits, plot their patterns in a horizontal plane, and tie them down to fixed co-ordinates; we could then go back and dig the ones which seemed most interesting. And since the preliminary test of the 'banjo' in 1966 had suggested that it would indicate quite small anomalies, we hoped to distinguish rock-cut features as small as post-holes. We might then predict, in advance of excavation, the plans of timber buildings.

This hope governed the actual pattern of our survey. Ideally, we might have exploited the continuous signal of the 'banjo' by walking it up and down a series of very close-set parallel traverses; putting a marker-peg in every time the needle dipped or rose; and then plotting, by normal survey methods, the anomalies which we had marked out. In fact this procedure would have been impossibly complicated and time-consuming, so we decided instead to set up a grid of twenty-metre squares, and to take readings at every half metre within these squares. The idea of such close readings was indeed revolutionary, for the standard practice at the time was to read at two metre intervals. The difference in effort is that between 121 and 1681 readings to a twenty-metre square, though this was partly offset by the portability of the 'banjo'. And, of course, we hoped that the effort would be more than repaid by the greater detail that we would obtain.

The geophysical reconnaissance: survey and results

Figs. 5, 6, 9

These, then, were the general considerations which controlled our programme of geophysical prospecting. In practice, we began in April 1967 with a three-week survey, covering the most level part of the plateau. Minor supplementary surveys were carried out during that summer; and having sampled the validity of the geophysical indications in the course of the 1967 excavations, we committed ourselves to a total geophysical survey. This was carried out during the excavation seasons of 1968, 1969 and 1970.

When we first went into the field with the 'banjo' in April 1967, it was still an untried instrument for archaeological prospecting: we were banking on faith, not certainty. To cover ourselves, we therefore arranged for a complementary survey with well-tried instruments and methods. The Oxford

Plate 6

Laboratory for Archaeology responded readily to our invitation, and a team under the leadership of Dr Martin Aitken joined us for a spell in April, and carried out further surveys both later that season and in 1968. The Oxford team brought a formidable range of instruments, both well-proven and newly developed: proton magnetometer, fluxgate gradiometer, and pulsed magnetic induction locator. It was particularly interesting to com-

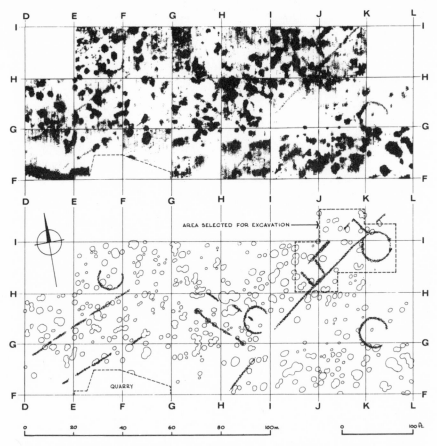

6 *Geophysical survey 1967. Dot-density presentation of the overall results of the Soil Conductivity Meter survey, together with an interpretation of the principal structures indicated by it and by the proton magnetometer. (See also Fig. 8)*

pare the results obtained by the various instruments. We also opened up three or four small cuttings in order to make sure that the geophysical anomalies really were related to archaeological features.

Field-work was only the first part of the geophysical survey. The next move was to convert columns of figures, which had no archaeological reference, into plots or drawings which suggested archaeological remains. The Oxford proton magnetometer measured anomalies against a more or less standard background, and in terms of an absolute scale of gammas. Consequently, its results could be plotted in absolute terms, and the most effective way to do this was to draw isographs joining up points of equal strength. The result looked like a contour-map, and we hoped that the contour patterns marked rock-cut pits and gullies.

I   Cadbury-Camelot seen from the air during the 1970 season of excavations. The circuit of Bank 1 is clear around the whole site; Banks 2 and 3 are visible at the south-east corner (compare Plate VII); but Bank 4 is shrouded by trees round the whole perimeter. The apparent banks in the left foreground are cultivation terraces, the so-called 'Linches'.

II   Early morning mists clearing to reveal the southern defences.

III   Excavation of the south-west gate in 1970. The road surface of the late sixth century AD has been uncovered, revealing evidence for the timberwork of the Arthurian gate-tower.

IV, V   Two stages in the excavation of a timber round-house in 1970. The building had originally been detected as a geophysical anomaly in 1967. For the geophysical plot, see *Fig. 6.* intersection of grid-lines K and G. For plans of the area, showing both circular and rectangular buildings, see *Fig. 11.*

I

II

III

IV

V

With the 'banjo', however, the flickering needle was not measuring any absolutes of conductivity or magnetic field. Theoretically, the instrument was tuned to a meter reading of 25 over undisturbed rock, and rock-cut features then registered as a lower reading, metal objects as a higher one. But changes in the bed-rock, along with signal-drift and the variability of the operators combined to make the background reading for any twenty-metre square vary from below 10 to over 30. (It was for this reason, above all, that various attempts to process the 'banjo' figures by computer all proved unsuccessful. Only in the final, 1970, season did we devise a new method of tuning and a new graduation for the meter-dial, which between them ironed out minor fluctuations of background reading and presented the rock-cut features which interested us in the form of positive readings.)

It was therefore necessary to examine every column of readings in order to establish the approximate background in each area. The strength of individual anomalies then appeared as the difference between the background and the actual reading. But two other facts had to be considered. The 'banjo' was reading not a point in the ground, but a hemisphere, more or less the shape of the radio signal between the transmitter and the receiver. Secondly, whereas our readings were at fixed half-metre intervals, anomalies were likely to occur quite randomly. The hemisphere of one reading might overlap the edge of a pit; that of the next might be central to it; that of a third might just clip the further edge. So in any visual presentation, the strength of anomaly registered at each station needed to be spread over the whole of the hypothetical hemisphere.

We made many attempts to devise an effective technique for visualizing anomalies. In the end my Deputy Director, Chris Musson, produced a series of dot-density drawings, in which dots were scattered around each reading-station. There was one dot for each point of difference between background and anomaly, and the dots were scattered randomly over the whole of the hemisphere that was being read. The procedure was lengthy and tedious, for up to twenty thousand dots were needed for each twenty-metre square. It also involved a certain intuitive feel and a great deal of artistry. The final plots, however, were strikingly effective. Examining them, I had the impression that I was looking at an archaeological site from which the top-soil had just been stripped, revealing a complex of pits, gullies, and other rock-cut features which only needed more precise definition by brush and trowel.

The dot-density presentation was visually spectacular; but did it really mean anything in either geophysical or archaeological terms? To answer

Figs. 6, 8 A

this, Chris Musson and I went to Oxford, where Dr Aitken's team had been plotting their figures. We laid out a mosaic which represented our dot-density version of the Cadbury summit plateau – a strip 60 metres wide by 160 long. On this mosaic the Oxford team then placed their contour plot. The two matched in almost every detail. It was important for our future surveys that the 'banjo' was thus vindicated. But for the present, what mattered most was that we could be sure that the Cardiff and Oxford plots together represented the geophysical pattern of the Cadbury summit. We had here a preview of the archaeological features, and an informed basis for planning our excavations in 1967. These must be the subject for the next chapter.

III   Excavation 1967–1968

Policy and organization

The account of our geophysical survey has taken me beyond the events which sprang immediately from the reconnaissance excavation of 1966. At the end of that season, after seeing the results, the Camelot Research Committee decided that it was justified in promoting a three-year campaign of excavations, on a scale that matched the potential of the site. From the archaeological point of view the Committee was influenced by our demonstration that ancient levels were still intact over much of the site despite centuries of ploughing; by our discovery that the defences had been rebuilt in the post-Roman centuries; by the recovery of Arthurian-period pottery in a potentially significant context; and by the increasing chronological range of finds. Moreover, the warmth of interest that the excavations had aroused encouraged the Committee to believe that a public appeal would raise funds on an adequate scale.

The first function of the Committee, then, was to find money. In practice, this devolved on the officers who had a busy time writing to learned societies and public bodies and organizing the distribution of an appeal to private individuals. A rough estimate suggested that we needed £15,000 for a three-year campaign. It was particularly useful that we obtained two large sums, from the Pilgrim Trust and the University of Wales, which were spread over the whole three years. Numerous other grants, both large and small, were also received, and we hoped to increase these by donations on the site and by the sale of picture post-cards of the dig and other literature. In the early summer, however, we were still well short of our financial target for 1967.

Meanwhile, the President and I, unknown to each other, had been negotiating for the sponsorship of national newspapers. His negotiations matured first, and so the Sunday *Observer* acquired exclusive rights to information during the 1967 season, in return for covering twenty per cent of our budget. Presumably the *Observer* hoped for sensational 'Arthurian' revelations; but in fairness I should stress that they continued to make grants in a wholly disinterested manner even after it had become obvious that there are few sensations or revelations in British archaeology. I personally shall always feel grateful for the firmness of their support at a critical moment in the planning of the 1970 season. The *Observer*'s claim to exclusive inform-ation was resented by some scholars, who quite erroneously thought that they were excluded. Less surprisingly, it caused hostility in the rest of the Press, and in later seasons rigorous 'exclusivity' was modified to 'most favoured treatment'. Some sensitive souls also found the *Observer*'s treatment of Cadbury distastefully trivial. They might usefully have reflected on the implication that the higher flights of scholarship are too remote for the readers of even a mature and responsible newspaper.

Apart from fund-raising, the Committee's other function was to approve the policy and programme of excavation, and the detailed budgeting, put before it by myself as Director. How was that programme and budget decided? I had determined the overall strategy of the excavation shortly after my appointment as Director. Looking at the numerous hillforts which had been excavated in southern Britain since the 1920s, I saw that they had yielded plenty of information about the construction and history of hillfort defences; a little about their gate arrangements; but almost nothing about what went on inside the defences. On the evidence available from most hillfort excavations, it was quite impossible to answer such obvious questions as: was the fort permanently occupied? by what size of population? at what kind of social level – peasants or warrior chiefs? was the fort a commercial, industrial or religious centre? To provide the evidence to answer these questions seemed a worthwhile objective; and the implication was that, although the defences and gates could not be ignored, our major effort should be concentrated on the interior of the fort.

With this policy there could be no disagreement, but the manner in which it was carried out provoked some dissent both inside the Committee and from outside. Granted that research should concentrate on the interior, there were almost eighteen acres to choose from. We worked principally

Figs. 9, 10

on the summit plateau. But the conventional view was that hillfort dwellers would have avoided 'windswept' summits, and would have placed their dwellings in a narrow zone in the lee of the ramparts. This belief was held because, although traces of houses are not normally visible in southern English hillforts, remains of them had certainly been recovered at the inner end of cuttings across the ramparts. It could be refuted, however, from the evidence of the hillforts of north Wales, where houses can still be seen today, spreading randomly over the whole interior.

At Cadbury, the air photos showed that storage pits covered the entire hill-top, and in 1966 substantial post-holes were discovered on the very summit. The geophysical survey started on the plateau because it was convenient to operate the instruments on level ground. Houses were certainly indicated, and thereafter we exploited the indications. The vindication of this policy of exploring the most level area of the hill will appear in Part II. But it is worth mentioning, as any hill-man knows, that the effects of wind on a hill are tricky. Sometimes air currents rise above the summit, leaving a sheltered zone in what appears to be the most exposed area. This is certainly the case at Cadbury, and the point is well appreciated by the modern denizens of the hill, a herd of Devon cattle, which always gathers on the summit on windy days.

So much for the overall policy. The more detailed planning for each season, the balancing of resources in money and manpower against the archaeological problems, was carried out by a Council of Supervisors. This consisted of the Director and Deputy Director, together with Site Supervisors, Finds Supervisor, and administrators, who met in Cardiff before each campaign, and held regular and formal meetings throughout each excavation season. Once a week during the dig, the Supervisors' Council was augmented into a Grand Council by the inclusion of everyone who had the slightest degree of responsibility. My role was simply to take the chair for discussions which ranged with complete freedom. The only limitations were those imposed by our actual resources of money and manpower – and in this field Chris Musson, as Deputy Director, kept a firm grip. There can be no doubt that the interchange of ideas and criticisms on the Supervisors' Council and the Grand Council contributed largely both to the effectiveness and to the sweet running of the excavation.

Plates 4, 5

Fig. 6

The excavation of the defences, 1967

Our excavation programme for 1967 had two aspects: to follow up the most promising geophysical indications on the plateau, and to cut a major trench through the defences from top to bottom. There was little difficulty in deciding where to locate this trench, for there were only two places, both on the south side of the hill, that gave clear lines through the trees. Cutting D, varying from two to five metres in width, was laid out on one of these lines, from the inner face of Ditch 1 across the three outer banks and the ditches between them. If the surveying of the defence profiles in 1966 had resembled jungle warfare, the excavation of Site D was often more like

Plates 14, 15, 27, 28, II

Fig. 21

65

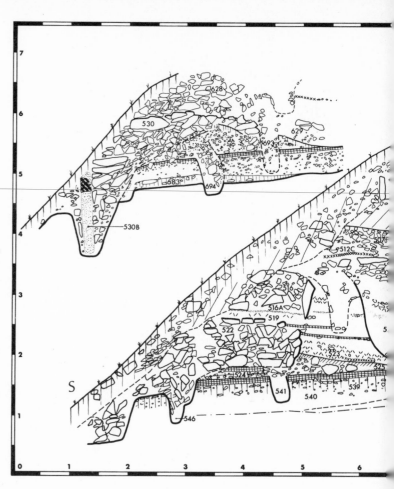

7 Bank 1: the stratification revealed on Site D in 1967–68. The principal defensive features are: 002 possible post-Ethelredan bank; 009, 020 two phases of Ethelredan bank separated by a spill of mortar; 010 Ethelredan mortared wall; 504,505 Arthurian-period Stony Bank, Rampart E; 506 probable refurbishing of Ultimate Iron Age defence, Rampart D, on eve of the Roman assault; 507, 512 tail of Rampart D; 513 paving at rear of secondary phase of Rampart C; 516, 628 early phase of Rampart C; 522, 530 body of Rampart B; 530 B front post of Rampart B; 693 rear post of Rampart B; 524 body of Rampart A; 546 front post of Rampart A, with ledge for plank revetment; 541,694 rear posts of Rampart A; 536 humus layer under earliest rampart; 539 stones of possible Neolithic bank. For reconstructions of Ramparts A and B, see Figs. 18 and 19

mountaineering than archaeology, so steep was the slope. Unfortunately the results did not match the effort. We could see that the outer banks had several distinct phases of building, but the scarcity of finds made it impossible to put close dates to these phases.

Research in the innermost rampart, on the other hand, was strikingly successful. Anticipating that the structural history of Bank 1 would be complex, we decided to take a quick preview of it by cutting a section parallel to the main trench by means of a mechanical excavator. It was a thrilling experience to have the history of the defences exposed within a couple of days of the start of the excavation. As a result, we formed an unduly favourable opinion of the value of such mechanical cuts; their limitations became manifest in 1969. For the present, we could see that Bank 1 incorporated at least five successive ramparts, rising to a height of sixteen or seventeen feet above the solid rock. And enough datable objects could be recovered from the layers exposed in the sides of the trench to show that there was a

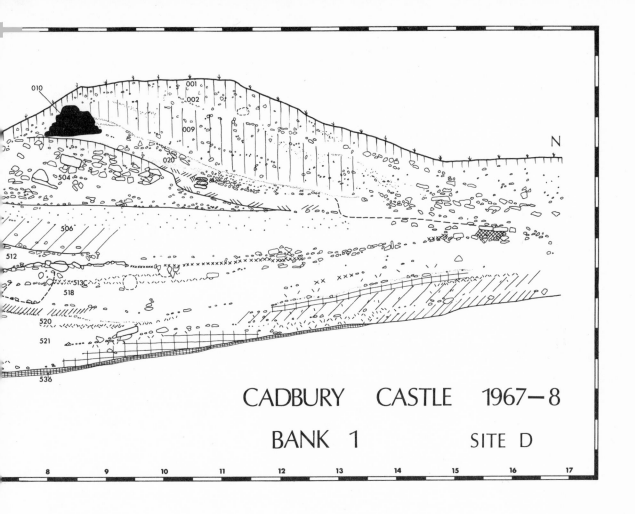

CADBURY CASTLE 1967—8

BANK 1   SITE D

distinctive rampart between the Ethelredan *burh* wall and the latest Iron
Age bank. This feature, christened the 'Stony Bank', was a candidate for an
Arthurian defence.

The results of the mechanical excavation were then followed up in detail
by hand-digging a trench ten metres wide. The late or post-Roman date of
the Stony Bank was confirmed by the discovery of Roman building debris
in its core. Structural details of the Stony Bank, and of the overlying Late
Saxon wall, were clarified. But work on these two ramparts proved so complex, and therefore so slow, that little time was left in 1967 to explore the
underlying Iron Age defences, which were likely to be at least as complicated. Several alternative plans of action were possible: to sacrifice details
in order to dig more rapidly through the Iron Age defences; to narrow our
cutting from ten metres to five or even less; or to postpone research on the
Iron Age until 1968. Pressure to sacrifice information to speed was resisted,
and the third policy was adopted. After reaching the top of the ultimate

Plate 73
Fig. 7

Fig. 5

Plate 81

Iron Age defence, we sealed it off with plastic sheeting and closed the trench.

As a compensation, however, we sampled the post-Iron Age defences in brief excavations on the other three sides of the fort – Sites A, I and J. These all produced evidence of the Ethelredan mortared wall, showing that it had a perimeter of about twelve hundred yards, and establishing Cadanbyrig as a medium-sized Late Saxon *burh*. Evidence for the Stony Bank was also found on both the east and west of the hill. On Site J, its date was carried into the fifth century or later by a stratified coin of Honorius, datable to AD 393–402. Even more important, on Site I a twenty-foot length of dry-stone wall was still in position, standing in places to a height of four or five courses. Gaps in the stonework showed where timber posts had decayed, and told us much about its structure. We shall see in Part Two that the discovery of the Stony Bank was a major event in Arthurian studies.

The prehistoric defences, 1968

Plates 38, 39

Fig. 7

The completion of our ten-metre cutting through Bank 1 was obviously a primary task in 1968. Because of the large area involved, responsibility was divided between two teams, one of them concerned with the ramparts proper, and the other with structures immediately behind the bank. Our work on Site A in 1966 had revealed drainage gullies and other traces of buildings behind Bank 1. This was, of course, in agreement with the evidence of other hillfort excavations, and with the general theory that Iron Age buildings should huddle in the shelter of the defences. Consequently there was some pressure from members of the Camelot Research Committee, and even on the Supervisors' Council, for a full exploration of this zone. But our results in 1968 were totally discouraging. With meticulous care, fragments of buildings were uncovered; but not a single coherent plan emerged. Moreover, the intensity of human activity, principally represented by black pits cutting into black soil, had left both structures and layers chaotically disturbed.

In the rampart proper, remains of structures were better defined: post-holes, rear walling, and paved rampart walks. But any trace of an outer revetment-wall eluded us for a long time. The problem here was that the forward slope of the rampart was a close-packed jumble of rubble, and it was difficult to know whether this was collapsed walling, or rampart core in position. It requires a degree of confidence to hack into this sort of tumble, and an even greater degree of discretion to know when to stop. In the end, I stayed on the site one evening after everyone else had gone – so that there

was no one to see my mistakes. After half-an-hour of precision hacking, I
had revealed the frail remains of what had once been a very beautiful wall-
face. Over the whole season we found traces of four or five distinct phases
of Iron Age rampart. Unfortunately the finds were few, so that it was not
easy to date these phases. Worse still, gaping holes and tunnels showed that
rabbits had burrowed right down to the earliest rampart, disturbing both
the finds and the stratification.

Plate 29

Our most unexpected discovery was an abundance of Early Neolithic
flints and pottery, which came both from pits and from an old ground
surface well below the earliest Iron Age bank. And at the very edge of the
slope, partly cut away by the construction of the first Iron Age rampart,
was a concentration of small rubble which hinted at a Neolithic bank. It
now seemed possible that we were going to find some kind of Neolithic
enclosure, similar in size to the Iron Age fort.

The south-west entrance, 1968

Our thorough exploration of the post-Roman defences in 1967 enabled us
to examine the contemporary phases of one of the entrances in 1968. Of the
two principal gateways, the south-western, or Sutton Montis gate, was the
obvious choice. To dig the north-eastern entrance would have cut our life-
line with South Cadbury village. Moreover, the Sutton Montis gate appeared
to have suffered less from erosion than the other one, and we already had a
little information about it from St George Gray's work in 1913.[21] In a small

Fig. 3

cutting at the inner end of the passage, he had located some rough walling,
and a road surface which apparently incorporated mortar. He believed that
this work was Iron Age, but our discovery of the Ethelredan mortared wall
in 1966 made it certain that what he had actually found was the Late Saxon
gate. We hoped to relocate this walling, and to expand outwards from
Gray's cutting, but the collapse and loss of stonework since 1913 made this
straightforward programme unworkable.

Our exploration of the gate was further complicated by the discovery of
a building-phase which we had not recognized in the ramparts in 1966 and
1967. We had reasonably expected that we would find the Ethelredan
mortared wall immediately below the turf, and we were encouraged by the
discovery of stonework poking up through the grass. When we uncovered
more of this, we found it was extremely massive: indeed, the corner stone
on the left of the gate was the largest building stone that we found anywhere
on the site. But this stonework was not mortared, so it was difficult to see

Plates 93, 94

how it could be Ethelredan. Eventually, we found remains of the *burh* wall buried beneath the massive unmortared wall. And reconsidering the rampart sections, we came to realize that a wall of similar character had been cut into the back of the Late Saxon bank.

When we uncovered the Ethelredan gate, we found that its actual remains were disappointingly slight, though the plan was clear enough. On the left

Plates 87–89

of the entrance passage, three or four courses of stonework were preserved, together with the footing course of the respond or pier for the gate itself.

Fig. 35

On the right, the walling had vanished almost completely. Between the passage-walls was a layer of soft mortar and rubble, which suggested the bed for a paved passage-way, but of actual paving there was not a trace. The slightness of what we found showed that the entrance had been very thoroughly demolished, and it is probable that this had been done on the orders of King Cnut, when he removed the mint from Cadanbyrig and abandoned the *burh*. This historical conclusion was some compensation for the poverty of the archaeological remains.

False clues in the interior, 1967

Fig. 36

When, in May 1967, we had found the Oxford and Cardiff geophysical surveys to be in complete agreement, we were encouraged to make predictions about archaeological features on the summit plateau. Apart from great numbers of blob-like anomalies, suggesting storage- or refuse-pits, there were also four or more circles or part-circles which were likely to indicate Iron Age round-houses. Even more interesting were three pairs of parallel lines, for it was reasonable to think that these marked close-set pits or even continuous trenches for the timber walls of rectangular buildings which were likely to be Arthurian or Ethelredan. This seemed especially probable in the case of the most easterly pair, for transverse lines were also visible, indicating, we thought, the two gables and an internal partition of a timber hall. This particular rectangle was immediately adjacent to a circle.

Fig. 8

The excavation of the two side-by-side would make a very convenient unit to control, so here, in 1967, we laid out the triple cutting E F G.

Plate 8

If the agreement of the Cardiff and Oxford geophysical plots had been exciting, the scene when E F G was stripped of top soil was even more thrilling. The correspondence between the dot-density plot and the visible archaeological features was almost complete. We felt that we had assisted at the birth of a new era in archaeological exploration, the electronic age. But our triumph was brief. Immediately after we had cleared the top soil,

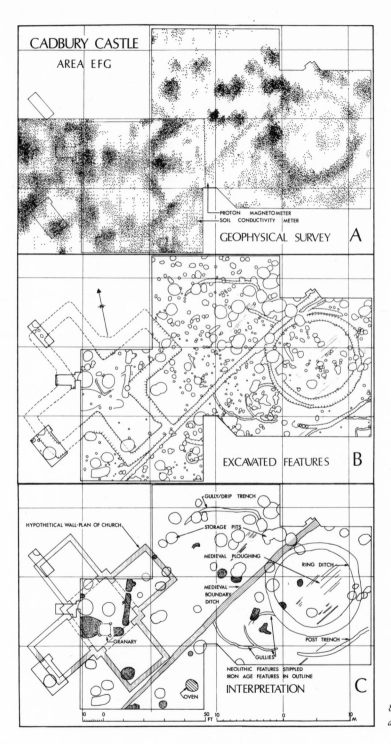

Within the figure:

CADBURY CASTLE
AREA EFG

PROTON MAGNETOMETER
SOIL CONDUCTIVITY METER
GEOPHYSICAL SURVEY **A**

EXCAVATED FEATURES **B**

GULLY/DRIP TRENCH
HYPOTHETICAL WALL-PLAN OF CHURCH
STORAGE PITS
MEDIEVAL PLOUGHING
RING DITCH
MEDIEVAL BOUNDARY DITCH
GRANARY
POST TRENCH
GULLIES
NEOLITHIC FEATURES STIPPLED
IRON AGE FEATURES IN OUTLINE
OVEN
INTERPRETATION **C**

10 0   50 10
                         FT
              0   10
                             M

8 *Geophysical survey and excavation of area EFG in 1967*

Plates 9, 41

Cadbury was swept by a torrential thunderstorm. The rain freshened up the contrasts in the soil, and revealed literally hundreds of small features – especially post-holes and gullies – which had not been visible before, and which had certainly not been indicated by the geophysical survey. After this, the 1967 season was a desperate race to examine and record all the visible features within the time-limits of the dig.

It was unnerving to uncover so many features which had not been picked up by the geophysical survey, especially as some of them were pits capable of holding substantial posts up to fifteen inches in diameter. We had expected that some small features might be missed between two reading-stations, even when these were only fifty centimetres apart; others might be blanketed by stronger anomalies near by. But we now had to admit that the chances of predicting timber buildings were slighter than we had hoped. Further dismay was caused when we found that even well-marked geophysical anomalies might be wrongly interpreted in archaeological terms. This was so in the case of each of the three 'halls'. A trial cutting across one line of the western 'hall' in 1967 showed that this was not a wall-trench but a field ditch. In 1968, part of the central 'hall' was cleared, and its apparent wall-trench was shown to be a chance alignment of refuse-pits. The 'hall' in cutting E F G proved the most curious of the three.

Even before excavation started, it was obvious that the anomaly which marked the more definite side of the eastern 'hall' extended well beyond the building, perhaps as a boundary fence. Excavation showed that it was in fact another field ditch, evidently representing a fairly recent phase of agriculture, for plough scratches could still be seen running parallel to it in the solid rock. As for the supposed transverse wall-trenches, the eastern gable turned out to be a casual alignment of pits, while the western gable and the internal partition developed into a shallow zig-zag trench utterly

Plate 90

unlike anything which any of us had seen before. Speculations about its function, both serious and frivolous, developed freely, until one day someone with a strong sense of pattern suggested that we had uncovered two arms of a cross. Probing with metal rods, followed by three small but precisely-sited cuttings, proved that this was correct. Our rectangle had become a cruciform trench.

It was then possible to see that this cross-pattern had already been indicated by the geophysical plot. But no-one would have dared to predict a cruciform building on the summit of Cadbury, whereas our speculations about a rectangular hall were altogether reasonable. The fact remained that the geophysical survey, even when misinterpreted in archaeological terms, had

led us to uncover a fascinating building plan, most probably the foundation   *Fig. 36*
trench for a Late Saxon church.

Iron Age pits and buildings

The geophysical survey had certainly been successful in locating the larger
rock-cut pits. Most of these had the organically-rich filling which was
expected to produce a strong magnetic anomaly. It seemed more surprising
that several Neolithic pits containing flints and pottery had also been detected,
despite the fact that their filling was free of organic matter. The reason was
that these pits contained a red clay, rich in iron oxides, and it was this which
was causing a detectable anomaly. In addition to the flints and Neolithic
pottery, the pits excavated in 1967 and later, yielded a rich haul of pottery,   *Plate 11*
bone and metal objects. Even the top soil in cutting E F G was prolific,
despite centuries of ploughing. Objects like a socketed bronze knife found
in 1967 strengthened our theories about a Late Bronze Age occupation; pins
of continental ancestry added an exotic element to the earlier Iron Age
phases; decorative bronzes revealed the artistry of later Iron Age metal-   *Plates VIII, IX*
workers.

So far as buildings were concerned, the geophysical survey had indicated   *Plates 40, 41*
several circular rock-cut trenches which had something to do with Iron
Age round-houses, and we explored one of these in cutting E F G. Un-   *Fig. 8*
fortunately, at the time we were left little wiser. No floor level or hearths
were preserved inside the ring-ditch; there was no apparent entrance, and
no convincing evidence to show whether the trench had held wall-posts,
or had been a drainage gully outside the house. There was even a suspicion
that the ditch had been abandoned in an unfinished condition. There were
also several narrower curving gullies, which might have held light timber
walling, or might have been drip gullies beneath the eaves of round-houses.
These represented further interesting structures which had not been indicated
by the geophysical survey.

This was why, when we were planning the 1968 campaign, we decided   *Fig. 5*
to follow up archaeological rather than geophysical indications. In the 1966
reconnaissance we had found traces of buildings, including burned wattle-
and-daub which seemed to have come from a house wall, beside the big
ditch on Site B. In 1968 we therefore laid out an area-excavation to explore
these traces. The results were so exciting that the cutting was rapidly ex-   *Plates 68, 69*
panded. The burned wattle-and-daub was in fact the remains of Late Saxon
ovens. Beneath these were curving scoops in the bedrock, which marked

Plates 4, 5

house platforms levelled off into the hillslope. If this interpretation was correct, then the 'big ditch' was a hollow-way or street, leading up from the north-east entrance, with house-emplacements either side. The rock here was a soft, even-surfaced sandstone, bright yellow in colour, in which stake-holes only a couple of inches in diameter showed up quite clearly. Some of the stake-holes marked an arc of the wattle-walling of a round-house which had been built in a very different manner from that in cutting E F G. Finally, there were two rectangular buildings, small in size but sophisticated in design, and laid out with regimented precision. These immediately suggested that a Roman garrison had been established at Cadbury just after the Conquest.

Arthurian possibilities, 1968

Plate 42

Fig. 10, 6

Our major cutting in the interior in 1968 was also based on archaeological indications obtained in 1966. When we re-examined the plan of Cutting C, it was evident that the four largest post-holes formed a rectangle, about sixteen feet by thirteen. In 1970 we came to realize that comparable structures were common at Cadbury, but at the planning stage in 1968 we thought it most probable that this rectangle was one element in a larger unit: just possibly the central feature of a circular house, more probably one bay of a large rectangular hall. Once again, we seemed to have an Arthurian or Ethelredan building in our grasp. We cleared an area all round the rectangle of posts and when the top-soil had been removed the bed-rock was seen to be honey-combed with the dark stains of rock-cut pits. At this stage of the excavation, it was not clear which of the pits had held posts and which were for storage or refuse. Accepting as a working hypothesis that all of them might have held posts, it seemed possible to trace rows of pits which incorporated the original rectangle as one element in a large hall. But as work progressed, first one and then another pit was eliminated, in the sense that it produced no recognizable evidence for a post. By the end of the season, we were left simply with a small rectangular building, closely surrounded with pits.

Plate 82

Fig. 5

Meanwhile, further east along the plateau, we were winning the first unambiguous evidence for an Arthurian structure. Hope triumphing over experience, we had laid out a small area cutting, Site L, across what was supposed to be one wall trench of the central 'hall'. As I have already said, what the geophysical survey actually indicated was a chance alignment of rubbish pits. Running at a slight angle to this, however, and not really

distinguishable on the geophysical plot, was a row of small posts set in a *Fig. 30*
narrow trench. Earth and gravel had been tamped around the posts to hold
them firm, and in this infilling were two fragments of a Tintagel-type
wine-jar. As it happens, the fabric of these jars is rather soft, so that when they Plate XIII
are broken the edges of the sherds are rapidly worn smooth. But the two
sherds from the post-trench on Site L had sharp, unabraded edges. They
must have been tamped into the filling shortly after they were broken. In
other words, the post-trench is contemporary with Tintagel pottery, and
broadly Arthurian in date. Consistent with this, there was a relatively high
concentration of such pottery scattered in the top soil of Cutting L.

Having found part of an Arthurian building, we had the urgent task of
tracing its whole plan. A slight curve in the line of posts suggested that they
marked either a curving gable wall, or possibly half one side – from gable to
doorway – of a boat-shaped building, which would have been appropriate
for a Dark-Age hall. But very strenuous efforts failed to produce clear
traces of the other walls of the building. The most that could be said was that
their structure must have been quite different from the row of small, close-
set posts which we had discovered. This was obviously a very tantalizing
note on which to end the 1968 season – but equally, the promise which it held
for future exploration was a great stimulus in planning our 1969 campaign.

IV Fulfilment 1969–1970

Policy and organization

When, late in 1968, the Supervisors' Council considered the past season's work, it became obvious that research at Cadbury could not be confined within the original three-year programme. The reasons were both archaeological and financial. Work on the south-west gate had already been put behind schedule by the discovery of a major post-Ethelredan phase; and it was impossible to believe that the Arthurian gate and four or more Iron Age precursors (to judge from the rampart sequence) could be examined satisfactorily in a single season. On the summit plateau, if we explored a major Arthurian building in 1969, we would need to search more widely for ancillary buildings in a follow-up season. In general terms, however much we might accomplish in 1969, it would still be necessary to dig for a further season in order to tie up the loose ends.

The financial case for a 1970 season arose from the fact that I was about to undertake a lecture tour in the United States in the Spring of 1969. My actual earnings from lecture fees would, of course, be available to help pay for the 1969 season; but the contacts which I hoped to establish in the States were unlikely to yield returns in hard cash before 1970. These reasons seemed cogent to those of us who were involved in the detailed planning of the dig. The landowners very readily assented to an extension of the work into 1970; and in due course, the Camelot Research Committee also agreed. Meanwhile, the work for the 1969 season was planned on the assumption that it would be brought to completion by a final campaign in 1970. Early in that year, a special appeal was launched to raise funds for the final season. It provoked a most generous response, most notably from public bodies like the British Academy, the Pilgrim Trust, and the University of Wales. And, in complete vindication of my optimism, there was a grant of five thousand dollars from the National Geographic Society of America, and a lesser one from the American Philosophical Society.

Two other important organizational changes were made in 1969 and 1970. In 1966, the decision to mount an excavation as well as a survey party

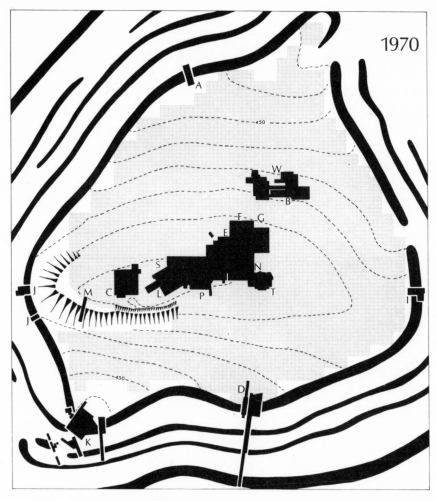

9 *The full extent of excavation (solid black) and geophysical survey (stippled) at the end of the 1970 season*

had been taken rather late, so it was necessary to arrange accommodation – beds, food and hot baths – at very short notice. We were very fortunate that one of our Somerset committee members, L. C. Hayward, was able to organize this for us at Chilton Cantelo School, about six miles from the dig. This had many advantages, but it meant that potential digging time was lost in travelling, and also that the dig administration had no direct control over our domestic comforts.

We therefore decided for our two final seasons to establish a fully equipped camp at the very foot of Cadbury. The decision was greeted with both welcome and opposition in the village of South Cadbury, and we gained some interesting insights into the workings of grass-roots democracy. Eventually, through the good offices of Mr and Mrs Montgomery, we found a superb site just below the northern defences, where it proved possible to lay out a well-equipped camp. The weary digger, dropping down to his tent or hut at the end of the day, looked out across the Somerset levels, and the romantics among us took spiritual refreshment from golden sunsets over Glastonbury Tor. The capital cost of the camp was high, but it was more than repaid by the improvement in both morale and actual working hours.

The second change concerned our personnel in 1970. In previous years our man-power had been very high, with over a hundred people at work at any one time. Sometimes, most notably in 1967, many of our volunteers were inexperienced, and supervisory skills had to be spread very thinly. In 1970, however, the absolute necessity of completing our research, and of doing so in good style, made it imperative to tighten up our whole organization. We considered that a team half the size of previous years, but consisting almost entirely of workers who had already proved themselves at Cadbury, could be far more effective than a larger team in which skill and commitment were both more diluted. The results completely justified this view. The hazards and fortunes of discovery made 1970 our most complicated and most exciting season. The highly-tempered research team which we had forged over the previous seasons proved itself fully competent to cope with the hazards and to exploit the fortunes.

The exploration of the Arthurian hall, 1969

Plates 16, 17, 83, 84

The first of the fortunes was a legacy from 1968: the exploration and definition of the Arthurian building indicated by the wall-trench containing Tintagel pottery. Immediately after this was discovered in 1968 we had tried to locate other parts of the building by means of limited but carefully sited cuttings. At the start of the 1969 season, we continued this policy of predicting the building plan, and then testing our hypotheses by selective excavation. But we were getting no result, and finally exasperation drove us to radical action. What we needed was to see a broad pattern. The post-trench was certainly part of a rectangular building: there must therefore be walls parallel to it, and others at right angles. If we cleared the bed-rock in a wide swathe at right angles to the trench, we must necessarily find other walls.

So we used a mechanical excavator to strip the topsoil in a band five metres wide and forty-five long. When the bed-rock was cleaned down, a row of post-holes appeared, in line with one end of the post-trench, and at right angles to it. This gave us one long wall, and incidentally demonstrated that our post-trench was an internal partition. We now knew the length and breadth of the building, and could lay out a cutting adequate to reveal its full plan. In point of fact the cutting revealed an appalling complexity of rock-cut features. In addition to ill-defined pits and gullies, these included the wall-trenches of two round houses; an arc of a ring-ditch; a ring of post-holes surrounding a hearth; storage and refuse pits of both Iron Age and post-Roman date; post-holes with Late Saxon pottery; and a medieval field boundary. There were also post-holes in lines either parallel to the post-trench or at right angles to it, and therefore potentially associated with it.

Fig. 5

The reduction of this chaos and complexity to order and simplicity was a two-fold process. Firstly there was the elimination of everything which could be shown, by associated finds, to be of a non-Arthurian date, and everything which was structurally out of character with the post-trench and the lineable post-holes. Then more positively, there was the definition of the post-holes which certainly or probably belonged together, either because they were similar in width, depth, or general character, or because they made sense in terms of plan and structure. Obviously there is a great deal of hypothesis-framing or model-making involved here. It will always be possible to dispute the attribution of individual holes, but despite this the general pattern of the Arthurian building was clear. Its size, over sixty feet by thirty, and its dominant position on the hill, show that it was the principal building – the feasting hall, in fact – of the Arthurian stronghold.

Fig. 30

Temples and workshops

The expansion of Site L to uncover the whole of the Arthurian hall was only one part of the continued exploration of the hill-top. By the end of the 1970 season we had examined about one fifth of the summit plateau, the central area of the fort and the most convenient ground for building. I have already explained the broad policy which underlay this. The detailed programme in 1969 was determined by the needs of Site L, and by the decision to seek more information about the Late Bronze Age and earliest Iron Age phases of the settlement. In 1967, finds of these periods had clustered most strongly towards the south of Site E F G, so this was expanded yet further south in

Plates 12, 13

Fig. 5

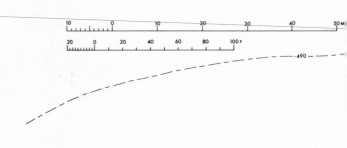

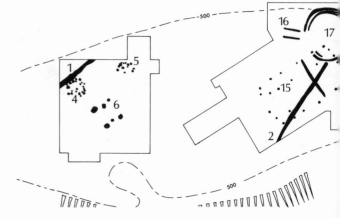

10 Principal structures revealed in the interior. 1–3 field ditches; 4, 5 post-hole clusters, perhaps house-sites; 6–14 six- (and four-) post buildings; 6 and 9 are possibly shrines; 15 Arthurian-period hall; 16 ancillary building; 17–21 ring-ditches of Iron Age houses; 22, 23 palisades and post-trenches, not certainly for houses; 24, 25 stake-built houses; 26 possible house-site; 27 porched shrine; 28 fence bounding zone of animal burials; 29 foundation trench of Ethelredan church; 30 probable Roman military buildings; 31 hollow-way

Plate 43

Fig. 9

Plates 45, IV, V

Cutting N. In 1970, we decided to fill the gap between Site L and the E F G N area with Cuttings P and S, and to expand around N in Cutting T. The last trench also involved an act of piety. The first geophysical anomaly that we had interpreted in archaeological terms was a ring-ditch on the eastern part of the plateau. One of our final acts in 1970 was to explore this anomaly in the eastern half of Site T. This proved to be one of the anomalies which gave a very precise prediction of an archaeological feature.

Our most remarkable discovery on Site N occurred in an area where the geophysical plot was blank. At the south-eastern corner of the cutting we

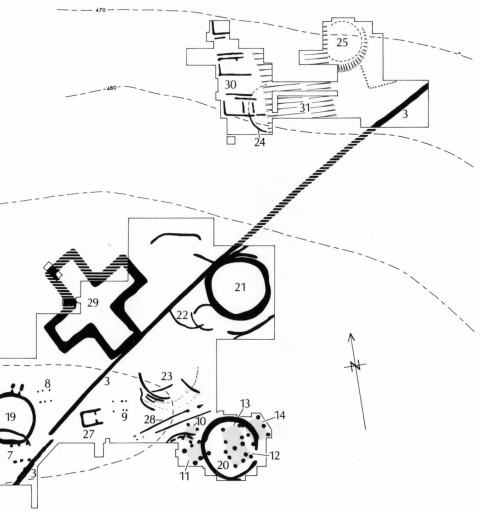

uncovered a well-defined rectangular wall-trench, which had held the
wooden uprights of a small square building with a deep verandah on the
eastern side. Large quantities of pottery, belonging to the very end of the
Iron Age, had been packed around the posts, so there was no doubt of the
date of the building. Granted an Iron Age date, the plan was unique in
Britain. In itself, it suggested a shrine, with an inner sanctum reserved for
priests and a porch where the profane worshipper might make his offerings.
Appropriately enough, in a narrow zone beside the approach to the shrine
we uncovered about twenty burials of young domestic animals: a few pigs,

Fig. 10, 27

Plates 46, 48

81

11 Structural analysis of post-holes and other rock-cut features on site T.

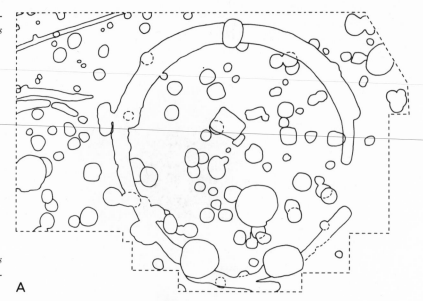

Outline plan showing all features uncovered by excavation, irrespective of depth, character and date. **A**

Three groups of Iron Age features are picked out: in light stipple, the ring-ditch of a round-house, and a pair of curving trenches possibly connected with another round-house; in heavy stipple, large storage-pits, some of them later than the abandonment of the round-house; and top-left, the fence-line bounding the zone of animal burials. The gap in the south-east perimeter of the ring-ditch probably marks the house-entrance **B**

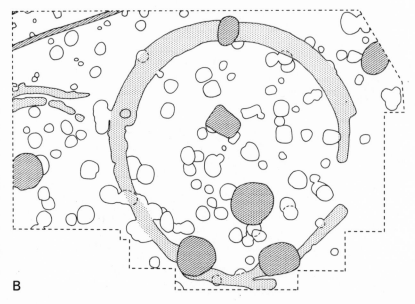

*The features picked out on plan B
have been eliminated from this plan.
The features which remain are: in
heavy stipple, Neolithic pits; in
outline, small or shallow pits and
post-holes; and in light stipple,
deeper pits capable of holding substantial posts for timber buildings.*

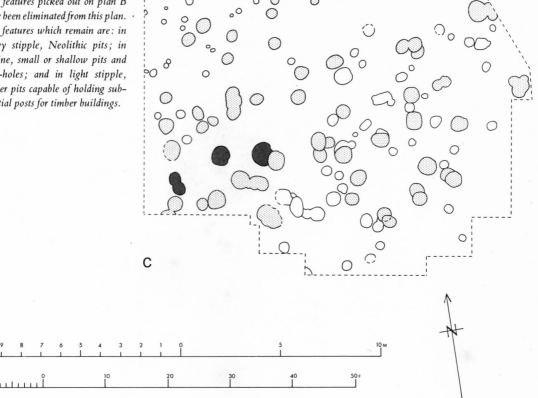

C

10 9 8 7 6 5 4 3 2 1 0   5   10 M

10   0   10   20   30   40   50 F

N

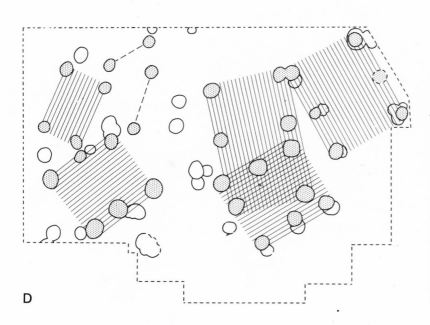

D

*Post-holes of comparable depth,
diameter and character fall into
four groups of six, one of four, and
two pairs. On this basis, five rectangular buildings may be inferred.
Overlapping lay-outs show that
not all these structures can have
been standing at the same time. On
the other hand, the multi-lobed
post-pits of the building on the
extreme right show that this had
been rebuilt several times, while
the pairing of post-pits on the
south side of the next building
shows that this too had been
rebuilt*

some lambs, but principally newly-born calves. Presumably the burials represented sacrifices in front of the shrine. These discoveries added a new dimension to our ideas about the function of hillforts. It had long been known that Romano-Celtic temples were built within derelict forts in the late third and fourth centuries AD, but this was the first positive indication of religious activity within a fort in the Iron Age.

Plates 47, 50, 63

North of the zone of animal burials, we found a surprising collection of ironwork, especially swords, daggers, and fittings from dagger-scabbards. Some of this weaponry had been disturbed by ploughing, so nothing could be learned from its actual position. One group, however, lay in a shallow pit, very similar to those which contained the animal burials, so this too may have been an offering at the shrine. On the other hand, some of the ironwork looked like scrap, and this was even more true of fragments of bronze from the vicinity. These included half of a bronze shield mount, decorated with elaborate Celtic scroll work. This is a major piece of Celtic art in its own right, and it gains added importance from being one of the very few objects of fine metalwork to come from a hillfort. Nearby was a group of furnaces, which we interpreted as an armourer's workshop on the evidence of the scrap bronze and iron. It may be that we have here two quite separate groups of metalwork, the one connected with ritual and the other with industrial activities.

Plates 51, 52
Fig. 22

Plate 55

Houses, circular and rectangular

The exploration of the summit plateau, and further work at Site B on the northern slope, also produced valuable evidence about domestic activity. One reason for exploring Site B was that stake-holes and other small features showed up very clearly against the smooth surface of the pale yellow sandstone. An arc of a stake- or wattle-built house had been discovered in 1968, but most of its plan had been lost in the big ditch or hollow-way.

Plate 53

Fig. 10, 25

Fortunately in 1969 and 1970 we were able to reveal the entire plan of a wattle-walled house, which had been built on a platform scooped into the hillside just to the east of the hollow-way. The discovery of this house-platform was particularly surprising in view of our conclusions in 1966. Evidently after the house was finally abandoned, the scoop had silted up with rain-washed soil to such an extent that there was not the least trace of it at the surface. On the air photographs and in the geophysical survey it had merged into the large, irregular blob of the big ditch. This explains why we had not predicted the house-platform before we discovered it by

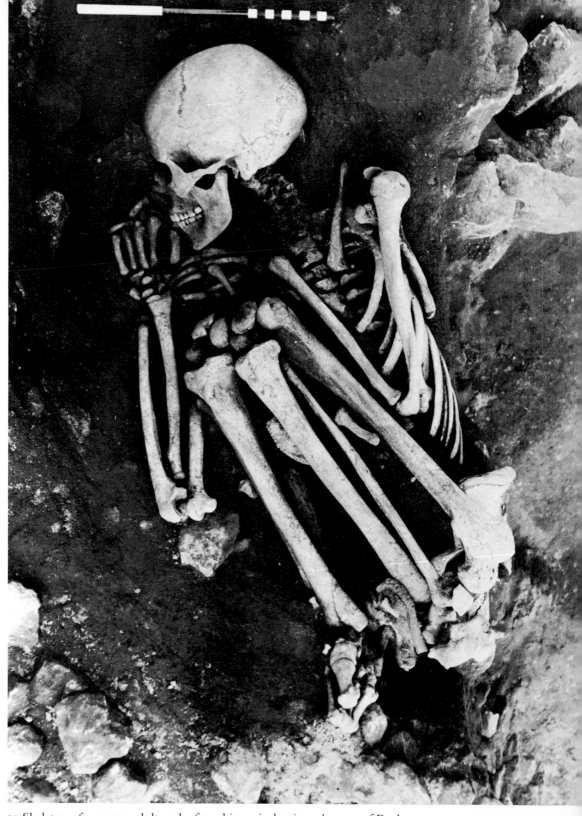

31 Skeleton of a young adult male, found in a pit dug into the rear of Bank 1 on Site I. There is no evidence for the cause of death, but the location of the burial suggests that it may have been a dedicatory sacrifice for the Ultimate Iron Age defence, Rampart D (pp. 102–3). Scale of centimetres

32 The final stage in the excavation of the south-west gate in 1970. All built walling has been removed, leaving only rock-cut features. In the background to the right of the upper two-metre pole is the floor of the earliest guard-chamber (p. 130). Thick black streaks in the side of the trench mark ash and charcoal lying on the upper floors of that guard-chamber. The lower ranging pole stands beside the hollow-way which developed during the Iron Age, in a massive pit which held one of the uprights of the Ultimate Iron Age gate (p. 162). The difference in height between the early guard-chamber floor and the Ultimate passage-way is an indication of the amount of traffic through the gate in the course of the Iron Age. Beyond the trench, the passage turns sharply to the right down the tree-filled gully

33, 34 Looking out through the Ultimate Iron Age gate (Fig. 12). To the right of the passage is the guard- ⟩ chamber, cut back into the rock in order to compensate for the wearing down of the passage-way. The bronze face-plaque was found on the guard-chamber floor (Plate XII). The double leaved gate was set at the point where the passage is narrowed by an offset in the walling on the left (most clearly seen in the lower view). The stone centre-stop for the gate can be seen in the passage at the near end of a pair of light coloured planks. Beyond the gate itself, the walling runs on to link up with the horn-work which can be seen behind the photographic tower. The large pit behind the left-hand passage wall held the door-posts of the middle-period guard-chamber; see Plate 35

35 One of the paired guard-chambers of the middle phase of the south-west gate (p. 134), that on the left-hand side looking out. The floor of the guard-chamber is already partly cut down into the rock to compensate for the wearing of the hollow-way, which lies across the bottom of the picture. The horizontal metre-rod lies on the actual floor; there are hearths of two periods in front of it, and a hoard of sling-stones to its right. The two vertical poles stand in a large pit which had at least two phases of use. It held posts for the door of the guard-chamber; for the gate itself; and for the timber revetment of the passage. Another revetment post stood in the right-hand pit

36, 37 Details of the gate arrangements of the Ultimate Iron Age gate. The upright stile of the actual wooden door had a massive iron spike driven into it, and was then bound with an iron collar to prevent splitting. The spike had a slightly domed head, which turned on a solid timber sill-beam lying partly across the passage and partly under the passage wall. The metre-rod stands in the rock-cut slot for the sill-beam. As the beam decayed, the spike and collar subsided to the position in which they were discovered. Just above them was found an iron key, while spear-heads, knives and fittings of uncertain purpose lay on the passage floor to the left. The whitening of the rock to the right of the metre-rod marks where the limestone blocks of the wall had been burned to lime in the final conflagration (p. 171)

38 The wall-trench (or drainage-gully) of an Iron Age round house discovered behind Bank 1 on Site A in 1966 (pp. 49, 68). The great depth of overburden made it impracticable to explore this further. The ranging poles are six feet long

39 Fragmentary dry stone walling, perhaps from an Iron Age building, uncovered behind Bank 1 on Site A (p. 49). Scale of inches and centimetres. The rounded stone in the middle course is not a discarded quern, but a disk or drum of chalk of unknown purpose

40 The excavation of the round house on Site G in progress in 1967. (*Fig. 10*, 21; p. 73). The ring-ditch probably held the timber uprights of the house wall. The post-holes within the ring-ditch have no apparent connection with the house. Compare Plates 9 and 41

41 The northern and eastern parts of Sites F and G at the end of the 1967 season. Iron Age storage pits in the foreground; field boundary-ditch and Iron Age ring-ditch in the background. (See also Plates 9, 40 and 90). All the major rock-cut features had been predicted from geophysical indications, but the smaller post-holes had not (pp. 70–2, *Fig. 8*). No coherent patterns have been recognized among the post-holes

42 Pits, post-holes, and a field ditch on Site C in 1968. The six-post shrine (*Fig.*> *10*, 6) is in the centre of the area, but cannot be distinguished in this view (pp. 136, 153)

43 The excavation of Site P in 1970. Beyond the central round house (*Fig. 10*, 19)> are the faint traces of another (*Fig. 10*, 18), and there is a clearer example to the right (*Fig. 10*, 17). See also Plate 44. The southern defences are in the background

44 The principal round house on Site P (*Fig. 10*, 19) completely excavated. In this case, the ring-ditch produced clear evidence that it had contained uprights in the form of split timbers, set side by side to form the house wall (p. 135). Outside the ring-ditch, at about four o'clock from the centre, are post-holes for a porch. The large pits around the house are storage pits, principally of the Late Iron Age, while some of the small holes held the posts of six-post rectangular structures like *Fig. 10*, 8

45 Site T in 1970. The penannular rock-cut ditch had been predicted on the basis of the first significant geophysical anomaly to be recognized in 1967 (*Fig. 6*). Excavation confirmed the existence of a ring-ditch for a round house with at least two building phases; and also revealed numerous storage or refuse pits, and post-holes for several four- and six-post rectangular buildings, most of which had not appeared as geophysical anomalies. For interpretative plans, see *Fig. 11*; see also Plates IV and V. In the right background are parallel fence lines (*Fig. 10*, 28), demarcating the area of animal-burials

46, 47 Details of Site N. The layer of fine cobbling, laid during an early phase of the Iron Age, has been cut into by the animal- and weapon-burials of the Late Iron Age (pp. 81, 84, 164). The animals were principally newly-born calves, but there were also some sheep and pigs. For the iron knife, dagger, and the scabbard plate which lies across it in three pieces, see Plate 50. It is remarkable that these objects, which lie just below the top-soil, have survived centuries of ploughing

48 Burial of the complete carcass of an ox immediately in front of the original six-post timber shrine (*Fig. 10*, 9) which lies just to the right of the standing figure. The wall-trench of the later porched shrine is in the background (pp. 80–1, 163–4)

49 Vertical photograph of the wall-trench of the porched shrine (*Fig. 10*, 27). One metre grid. The trench which would have held the wooden walls of the shrine, contained pottery dating to the last decades of the Iron Age

50 Iron objects from the weapon-burials on Site N (p. 84). Ring handles from cauldrons, a leaf-shaped spear-head, a knife, a dagger blade, and scabbard plates, chapes, and bindings; see Plate 47 for some of these objects *in situ*. The dagger is $15\frac{1}{4}$ ins long

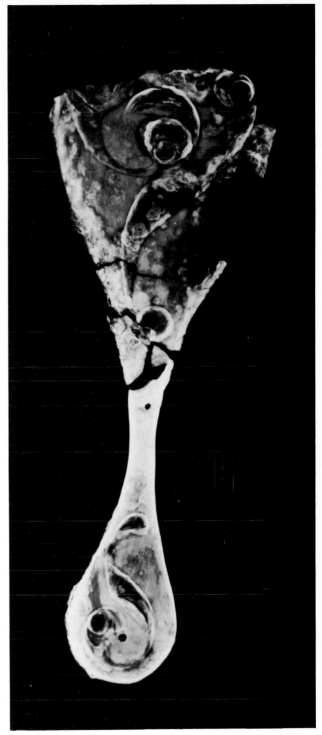

51, 52 Bronze fragments comprising about half of a mount from an Iron Age shield, with a repoussé ornament of bosses and scrolls in the La Tène (Celtic) art style (pp. 84, 154). The photos show the fragment as it was found, badly defaced by corrosion; and under treatment in the British Museum, an X-radiograph which reveals the decoration more clearly. Overall length of the fragment 7 ins. For a reconstruction of the shield see *Fig. 22*

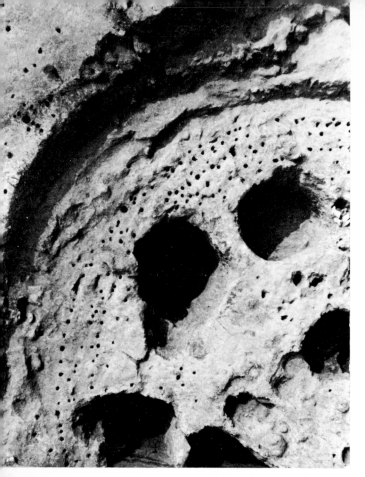

53 Near-vertical view of the stake-built round house set on a platform levelled into the northern slopes of the hill on Site B (*Fig. 10*, 25; pp. 84, 135). There are four or more concentric rings of stake-holes, indicating that the house had been rebuilt several times on the same site. It is not certain that the large storage pits are contemporary with the house

54 Ox-skull laid on a bed of stones at the bottom of a rock-cut pit on Site C (pp. 74, 136, 153)

55 The metal-working area on Site N (pp. 84, 156). In the foreground, beneath the one-metre rod, is a hearth of level slabs; in the right background is a complex of hearths or furnaces surrounded by vertical slabs

excavation. It was nevertheless disturbing that such a major alteration of the bed-rock had merged so completely into the general slope of the ground.

On the plateau we uncovered a number of circular structures. On the whole, the rock of the plateau was too irregular to allow us to define features as small as stake-holes, though in one area a faint curving groove in the rock did mark the last vestige of a round-house. Elsewhere a compacted spread of fine cobbling had, very surprisingly, escaped destruction by ploughing, and arcs of stake-holes could be detected both in the cobbling and below it. But normally the Iron Age houses appeared as clear-cut gullies or trenches in the solid rock. These had originally held timber walls, but very little evidence was preserved to show either the size or arrangement of the timbers. Another disappointment was that, out of all the houses located by excavation, less than half had been indicated by the geophysical survey.

Plates 46, 47

We had, of course, confidently expected to find circular wooden houses at Cadbury, because these are normal on British Iron Age sites. Indeed, in recent decades the belief had grown up that, whereas their continental ancestors had always built rectangular houses, the Iron Age Celts of Britain had built only circular ones. From the time when it was first formulated, it was possible to show that this was a gross over-simplification. And from the early 1960s, the realization had been growing that in some hillforts the only residential accommodation had been in small oblong buildings, while round-houses were lacking. At Cadbury, the six-post building found on Site C in 1966 had appeared to be completely isolated; but in 1969, and to an even greater extent in 1970, we were able to show that clusters of post-holes of distinctive depths and character could be arranged into rectangular four- and six-post patterns. As with the Arthurian hall, the elucidation of these structures out of a great confusion of pits and post-holes was as much a matter of elimination as of establishing positive characteristics. Rectangular six-posters were particularly common on Site T, where they appeared to be earlier than a circular house, and probably earlier than the cobbling as well.

Fig. 10, 6

Fig. 11

The rectangular building-trenches discovered on Site B in 1968 were quite a different matter. Our work in 1969 helped to emphasize their regular, even regimented, lay-out. In terms of finds, these buildings could be dated to the very end of the Iron Age, or to any later phase in the history of Cadbury. But it was difficult to believe that anyone other than Roman soldiery would have set out their buildings with such precision. So it was no surprise when sixty feet away, just across the hollow-way, we found a Roman field oven. With it were various discarded bronzes which showed that a military unit had been repairing armour and other equipment damaged in battle.

Plate 69

Fig. 10, 30

Plates 70–72

101

The defences in 1969 and 1970

Fig. 5

The spectacular success of the mechanical cut across the ramparts in 1967 encouraged us in 1969 to excavate four more trenches by machine. Two of these, A and I, were intended to carry pre-existing cuts down to bedrock; J '69 replaced J '67, in what was thought to be a better position; and K was located beside the south-west gate in order to preview the Iron Age stratification there. While we knew that the cost of hiring a digger and dumpers would be high, we believed that the expense would be more than justified by the additional evidence we would win about the construction and history of Bank 1. And we had two more specific problems in mind as well. In 1968, we had found only two sherds of pottery which were relevant to the date of the earliest Iron Age rampart. It was reasonable to hope that four further cuttings might increase this evidence. Secondly, we wanted to look on all sides of the hill for further traces of the Neolithic bank which we had found at the head of the slope in Trench D.

In fact, this programme ran into many difficulties. In Cutting A, the digger had to be laid off because it was scooping out a pit containing interesting timber-work and pottery. On Site I, it was stopped, almost miraculously, as its bucket scraped the skull of a human skeleton. And apart from particular incidents of this kind, we were left with deep reservations about the value of machine cuttings across complicated ramparts like Bank 1 at Cadbury. Mechanical digging necessarily destroys most of the evidence in plan – and this includes, for instance, defensive walls. Bearing in mind that all archaeological excavation is a destructive technique, this degree of destruction is justified if the evidence can still be clearly seen in the sides of the trench, and can be interpreted there. But when a dry-stone wall is sliced through by the digger, the stones which comprise it frequently drop out of the face of the cutting. Nothing in the way of coherent structures is left behind, and rational interpretation becomes almost impossible.

Despite these limitations, some interesting information was salvaged from the mechanical cuts. A further phase was added to the history of Cadbury by the discovery of a large part of a Late Neolithic pot at the very bottom of Trench A. Close by was a stake-hole, hinting at a Late Neolithic house or other structure. Unfortunately, it was impracticable to remove fifteen feet of overburden, in the form of the Iron Age ramparts, in order to explore this level extensively. In Cuttings A, I and J no trace was found of a Neolithic bank comparable with that suspected in D. In fact, no Early Neolithic material of any kind was found in these trenches. The mechanical cut in K did yield a few sherds of Early Neolithic pot, and some contemporary flints,

Plate 31

Plates 21, 22
Fig. 14

but there was not even a hint of a bank associated with them. Consequently, in my interim report on the 1969 season, I wrote off the idea of an enclosed or defended hill-top settlement in the Neolithic period. But the hypothesis was revived in 1970, when we found beside the south-west gate a rock-cut ditch, K618. This was over eight feet wide and four feet deep, and had a red clay filling which we considered characteristically Neolithic.

For the Iron Age, the most interesting discovery was a human skeleton on Site I, for this was the only regular burial to be found in Iron Age Cadbury. Even this can scarcely be counted as a normal burial. A young man, with no signs of physical defects, had been crammed head down into a small pit in the back of Bank 1. Another phase of rampart-construction was then built on top. The general character of the burial suggested that it was a dedicatory sacrifice intended to bless the later rampart.

Plate 31

Apart from its intrinsic interest, the skeleton was important because its presence forced us to abandon the mechanical excavation of the front half of Trench I. In the course of completing the excavation by hand-digging, we discovered clearly-defined lines of stones running through the Arthurian-period defence. These showed us where a framework of heavy timbers had rotted away. The frame had been constructed of horizontal beams, running both parallel to the rampart face and at right angles to it, which were slotted in to front and rear rows of upright posts. Similar evidence for wooden beams had been found in Cut D in 1967, but at that time they appeared to be a purely local feature, and they were therefore interpreted as evidence for a tower. Now, however, we realized that elaborate timber framing was a regular feature of this phase of Bank 1. So, piece by piece, a complete picture of the Arthurian defence was appearing.

Plate 74

The elusive Arthurian gate

At the south-west entrance, our programme for 1969 and 1970 was to explore the Arthurian gate and the last of its Iron Age precursors in 1969; to protect the remains with plastic sheeting and turf during the winter; and to complete the excavation of the Iron Age gates in 1970. Bearing in mind other final seasons on Iron Age gateways, notably that at Maiden Castle, Dorset, in 1937, I had no doubt that our last season would be protracted. But I was determined that the exploration of the gate should be completed satisfactorily and in this I had the support of a devoted team on the site itself.

Much of the 1969 season was taken up with expanding the scale of our operations at the gate, which in 1968 had been largely confined to the en-

Plates 87–89; *Fig. 5*

Fig. 35

trance passage itself. One of our particular problems was how the Ethelredan gate was placed in relation to the perimeter. At one stage of the work it seemed likely that the gate was set forward from the wall in a projecting tower, and extensive clearance was needed to disprove this idea. A major difficulty in working in the entrance was that some six feet of soil had accumulated since the Ethelredan period. The removal of this was just a hard slog, devoid of any interest, but fortunately we were able to improve both mechanical efficiency and morale by installing a small crane.

Towards the end of the 1969 season, we came to believe that the building of the Ethelredan gate passage had destroyed most of the evidence for the Arthurian gate. On the right of the passage, no pre-Ethelredan stonework was preserved. On the left, there was a short row of walling which had the same character as the wall-face of the Stony Bank which had been uncovered on Site I in 1967; that is to say, Roman dressed stone was re-used in a timber-framed dry-stone wall. There was no doubt that this was the Arthurian wall-face, but there appeared to be no gate structure or road-way associated with it. The walling broke off towards the passage-way, and the first detectable road surface was some twenty inches below it. This well-laid cobbling was attributed to the end of the Iron Age, and we believed that the Arthurian gate and road had both disappeared. The 1969 season ended on this note of disappointment.

Plate 76

Plate 75

In 1970 we began by removing the protective covers, and then cleaned up the supposed Iron Age cobbling. Our first move into new ground was a small exploratory cut across the road. Immediately we found, among the cobbles, an iron axe-hammer of Roman or later date; and beneath them, a silver ring or buckle with Anglo-Saxon ornament of the sixth century A D. A drastic revision of our previous ideas was forced upon us. The cobbled road, far from belonging to the early first century A D, could hardly be earlier than the late sixth century. How did the road relate with the supposed Arthurian walling? Was there evidence for an Arthurian gate still to be found?

Plates 79, 80, XI

After much painstaking dissection, we concluded that the sixth-century gate had been a timber structure. Where the rampart butted against the gate, it had been shored up with wooden planks; and the decay of these explained why the walling appeared to be broken off. As for the difference in level between the road-way and the walling, this was the result of the road being laid in a hollow-way formed during the Iron Age. In addition to the timber planks shoring up the rampart ends, there were heavy timber sill-beams or thresholds across the passage at the front and rear of the gate. At either end

Plates 77, 78, III

of the thresholds, dark stains showed where stout corner posts had decayed. We were able to follow these down, and to show that the uprights had been deeply bedded, in three cases down to the solid rock. From this, we inferred that the gate had risen to a good height as a look-out tower or fighting plat- *Fig. 29* form. Finally, by carefully peeling off the late sixth-century road, we were able to show that this represented a refurbishing or repair to an earlier road. It was a reasonable inference that the first road, the timber gate through which it led, and the dry-stone and timber defensive wall, all belonged to that late fifth- or early sixth-century occupation which was already known from the occurrence of Tintagel-type pottery. Here then, after all our early disappointment, was the Arthurian gateway of Cadbury-Camelot.

Massacre and defence

The interest and excitement of the 1970 season at the gate was far from ended, however. The same trial cutting which had contained the silver ring and the iron axe also produced, when it was deepened, brooches and weapons of the Ultimate Iron Age; then fragments of human skull; and then a human *Plate 67* leg, complete from the toes to the head of the femur, but with no body attached to it. These were the first hints of the richest and most macabre archaeological deposit I have ever excavated. Down the length of the Ultimate Iron Age passage-way were scattered well over a hundred bronze *Plates 65, 66* brooches – some of them broken, but others still in working condition. Then *Plates 36, 63; Fig. 26* there was a large collection of iron pikes and javelins, indicating a battle between native defenders and Roman assailants. But the most striking object was a bronze plaque, in a very frail condition, which was lying face down- *Plate XII* wards under the wreckage of the guardroom roof. The plaque had to be strengthened with bandages and plastic resin before it could be lifted. When it was turned over it revealed a face, human or divine, in a style that was an ambiguous mixture of Roman realism and Celtic stylization.

As for the bodies, there were fragments of about thirty men, women and *Plate VI* children, in every imaginable state of dismemberment, strewn along the passage. So gruesome was the scene that some of our volunteers refused to work there. Curiously enough, only one bone showed any sign of battle injury. This was the ulna – one of the bones of the forearm – of an adult, which had been chipped perhaps in trying to ward off a sword blow. Apart from this, there were no signs of weapon cuts, and the fragmentary state of the bodies was not the result of their being hacked to pieces. It seemed probable that after a battle and massacre, the corpses of the defenders had

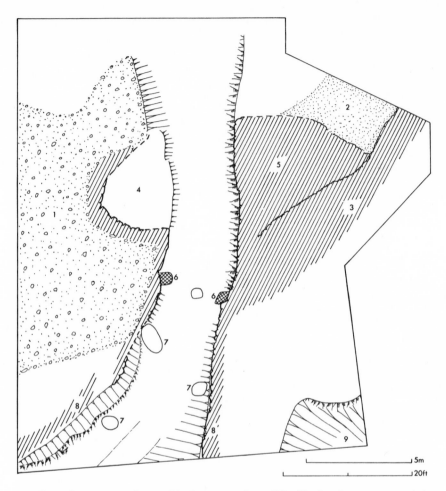

12 *The south-west gate on the eve of the Roman assault. 1 rubble of Bank 1, front revetment missing; 2 gravel tail to 3 wall of massive stones, front revetment missing; 4 stone-walled guard-chamber, partly excavated out of the solid rock; 5 rubble infilling of earlier guard-chamber; 6 timber beams supporting the two-leaved gate, hole for door-stop between them; 7 large pits holding uprights for barricades used to block the entrance at the time of the assault; 8 link-walls between Banks 1 and 2; 9 butt-end of Ditch 1*

been left unburied. They were then pulled to pieces by wolves and other wild beasts. Some time later, the Roman troops returned to destroy the defences, and the timber-work of the gate was burned down over the pitiful remains.

When the last brooch and spearhead had been collected, and the last human torso had been photographed and removed, we had before us the remains of the south-west entrance as it had stood on the eve of its over-

Fig. 12

throw by the Romans: a stone-lined passage, with a single guard-chamber on the left-hand side. A very remarkable feature was that there was no made road through the entrance. The living rock itself formed the road surface, and this was heavily rutted by cart-wheels. Moreover, during the centuries of Iron Age usage, the rock had been worn down by the passage of feet, hooves and wheels, until a hollow-way over six feet deep had been formed. To cope with the progressive deepening of this passage-way, successive guard-chambers had been cut down into the rock beside the entrance. Normally speaking, of course, later structures lie on top of earlier ones, but here, the stratification was completely topsy-turvy: the floor of the earliest guard-chamber was at about the level of the eaves of the latest one.

Plates 33, 34

As a result, of course, the intellectual task of disentangling the history of the Iron Age gate was extremely complicated. The physical work of exploration was heavy too. During the middle phases of the gate's history, there had been a guard-chamber on either side of the entrance, but as the passage became progressively deeper it was decided to wall off one guard-chamber, and fill it in with many tons of rubble. All this, of course, had to be removed before the earlier phases could be examined. We were sustained, however, by a continued sense of excitement and achievement, for gateways of this scale and complexity have not often been explored in Britain. There was an aesthetic stimulus, too. Everyone has heard of the glowing colours of the desert city of Petra. The bedrock of the south-west corner of Cadbury is a golden-brown, turned crimson in places by the conflagration that had ended the Iron Age. During a spell of superb autumn weather, these colours were warmed by the evening sunlight until Cadbury-Camelot itself seemed a 'rose-red city, half as old as time'.

The weather broke, though the spell lasted. As every archaeologist has experienced, the time set aside for final surveying saw high winds and heavy rain. But at last every rock-cut pit and gully was on the plan, and the final melancholy operation of back-filling could begin. Five strenuous seasons of fieldwork were at an end: equally arduous work in study and drawing-office and laboratory lay ahead. It is time now for us to turn from exploration to results.

V The earliest settlements:
Neolithic, Bronze Age, Earlier Iron Age

The enigmatic Neolithic phases

Part One, in describing how we explored Cadbury-Camelot, will already have given the reader some idea of the richness and complexity of our discoveries. In Part Two the results of our explorations are summarized. The best thread to guide us through the complexities is obviously a chronological one, so I begin at the far end of the long vista of human activity on Cadbury hill. It is unfortunate that this makes it necessary to start with the most shadowy and enigmatic phases, but we may recognize that their very obscurity is a product of their remoteness in time.

Plate 11

This is not to say that actual objects of the earliest period are all equally difficult to recognize. On the contrary: the characteristic flint arrow-heads of the Early Neolithic have often been picked up by collectors when the site has been under plough. Equally characteristic, and readily recognizable, are the axe-heads which had been chipped out of flint nodules or lumps of fine-grained igneous rocks, and then polished to a cutting edge. These axes look clumsy when compared with the metal axes of later cultures, but modern experiments have shown that they are quite effective for cutting down small trees, or ringing larger trees to kill them. Once the tree is dead, it may be burned down, and a fruitful crop may be raised from the ashes. This slash-and-burn agriculture was introduced to these islands by the first farmers along with other aspects of Neolithic culture. The axes from Cadbury are evidence for forest clearance and farming, but not necessarily for a settled occupation of the hill.

The arrow-heads likewise are not evidence for settlement, but for the hunting of small game through the primeval forest, or across the cleared fields. Even when we find the flint scrapers used for cleaning skins, we can still infer nothing more than the activities of a hunting party. But the sure clue to more permanent occupation is provided when we find axes, arrow-heads, scrapers, and waste from their manufacture, all associated with Early Neolithic pottery. For though there is equivocal evidence that such pottery was traded, for instance from Cornwall to Wessex, it is not likely that it was carried around by hunting parties. In the collections of Mrs Harfield and J. Stevens Cox, a considerable amount of pottery was attributed to the Neolithic on the evidence of the grits in the clay and the form of the vessels.[21] Now, however, that the great variability of Iron Age pottery from Cadbury is fully appreciated, we might feel more doubtful about claiming a Neolithic date for sherds collected from the surface.

There can be no similar doubt about the pottery found during the excavations, actually associated with arrow-heads and other flints, in pits with a characteristic filling of red clay. The vessels are principally open bowls, hemispherical or deeper, with thin walls, and rims which have been thickened for ease of handling. Some bowls have tubular protrusions on the side, probably to take a cord for hanging the vessel. It is difficult to believe, however, that they were ever suspended over an open fire as stew-pots, for they would have cracked apart with the heat. These suspension tubes – trumpet lugs to give them their technical name – are seen again on pottery from sites like Windmill Hill in Wiltshire, Maiden Castle in Dorset, and Hembury in Devon.[22] Along with other less distinctive features, they relate the Cadbury vessels to a broad class of Early Neolithic pottery well known in southern and south-western Britain.

Fig. 13

Little can be said about the structural features of the settlement which used this pottery. In 1967 a straight-sided gully containing Neolithic material was found on Site E. At its southern end was another Neolithic feature which appeared to mark a right-angled return. It seemed very likely, on the evidence then available, that we had one corner of a fenced enclosure, or even of an actual building. But wider exploration in 1969 failed to produce any comprehensible continuation of these gullies. We are left, then, with the pits, which occurred both on the summit plateau in E F G and P and more rarely in N and T, and also under Bank 1 on Site D. The most obvious feature distinguishing these pits from those of the Iron Age was their filling. Whereas the later pits normally had a black, dark brown or even greenish fill, obviously enriched with organic matter, the Neolithic pits contained a clean red or reddish brown clay. A similar red clay was preserved under the earliest rampart, where it was clearly a product of the natural weathering of the limestone bedrock. In other words, before human activity began at Cadbury, the natural soil would have been this red clay, with a thin covering of humus or leaf mould from the primeval forest. The first inhabitants cut their pits through the clay and into the solid rock, and subsequently filled more or less clean clay back into the hole.

Fig. 8, C

Fig. 7

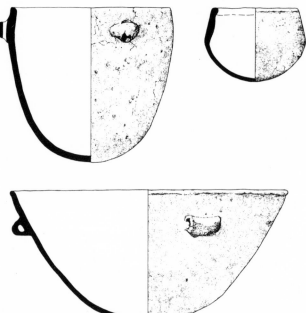

13 *Restored examples of Neolithic pottery of Windmill Hill type. The largest bowl has trumpet-lugs and is 6¾ ins deep*

Plates 18–20

What was the function of such pits? A good example, rich in finds, was the one recorded as P154. This contained sherds from several pottery bowls; a couple of flint arrow-heads, and a large number of waste flakes; ribs and other bones from an ox; part of a red deer antler; burned hazelnut shells; and a human lower jaw. Were it not for the arrow-heads, which were complete, and the human jaw, this might look like domestic refuse. Pit C817 contained only part of a human skull and clean red clay; while another pit contained simply red clay and waste flakes of flint. It is difficult to provide any rational explanation for such pits. Not surprisingly, the archaeologist takes refuge in quasi-explanations in terms of ritual. The pits had been dug – and promptly re-filled, if we may judge from the cleanness of the clay – in order to make offerings to some Earth Mother or other deity. Unsatisfactory though it is, this is the best explanation that can be offered.

What was the character of the settlement containing these mysterious pits? Windmill Hill and Hembury belong to a class of site known as 'causewayed camps'. That is to say, a hill-top or promontory had been enclosed by concentric ditches which instead of being continuous were interrupted by numerous causeways. The purpose of these enclosures is obscure, but they may have been seasonal meeting places, the sites of fairs and religious festivals. Whatever the true explanation of Windmill Hill and Hembury, there is no evidence from air photography or geophysical survey that the summit of the Cadbury hill had ever been the site for such interrupted concentric ditches. Indeed, there is nothing to show that the Neolithic settlement had been enclosed by any kind of ditch or bank, for we shall see in a moment that the ditch with 'Neolithic' red clay filling, K618, which we discovered in 1970, was actually a work of the Bronze Age. In fact, on the available evidence, Neolithic Cadbury consisted simply of a bare hill-top with 'ritual' pits scattered here and there. Unenclosed hill-top settlements of Neolithic date have occasionally been explored in the past, notably at Hazard Hill in Devon.[23] There, as at Cadbury, no Neolithic buildings could be recognized, nor could the purpose of the settlement be determined. The most we can say is that these are characteristically Neolithic enigmas.

Dating the Early Neolithic phase

So far nothing has been said about the date of the Early Neolithic occupation. A generation ago, this phase in the British archaeological sequence had to be dated by dead reckoning backwards from the end of the Neolithic and beginning of the Bronze Age. That event itself was fixed by comparing British Early Bronze Age objects with similar pieces in western Europe, which in turn were dated by comparisons in Central Europe and the Mediterranean, through to Egypt where a chronology in terms of years was established on the basis of the known dates of the pharaohs. Accepting all these comparisons, the Neolithic was thought to end about 1500 BC, and to begin about 2000 BC, but it was recognized that there were many tenuous links in the chain of inference. Consequently, archaeologists were greatly pleased when, in the late 1940s, the problem of dating early sites was taken out of their hands by the development of various scientific techniques. The best known of these, the radio-carbon or Carbon-14 technique, is now the basis for our Neolithic chronology. But before we state the results of C-14 dating at Cadbury, it would be as well to set out for the lay reader some of the limitations inherent in the method.[24]

Radio-carbon dating is based on the observation that all living things contain a minute quantity of radio-active carbon, which is maintained during the life-time of the organism, but which decays very slowly on its death. Assuming that the rate of decay is constant, if the radio-activity still remaining in an ancient animal bone or piece of wood is measured, this should indicate how long ago the animal died or the wood was cut from its parent tree. The first limitation is that the method of measuring the remaining radio-activity is a statistical one and the result is a statement of probability, not of certainty. A Carbon-14 date for a British Iron Age site might be expressed, for instance, in the form 450 BC $\pm$ 150 years. If this meant that the date is probably 450 BC, and must certainly be within the bracket 600–300 BC, it could be helpful. In fact, because of the statistical method, all that is meant is that there is a 2:1 chance that the date falls somewhere between 600–300 BC, and a 19:1 chance that it lies between 750 and 150 BC. Closer limits than $\pm$ 150 years are indeed possible, but there are reasons for doubting whether they can be refined to less than $\pm$ 100 years. Since the cost of a C-14 test is not cheap, some workers in the Iron Age prefer to spend their limited funds on more digging. No C-14 samples were taken from Iron Age levels at Cadbury.

With the Neolithic of western Europe and the British Isles, however, where other methods are lacking, radio-carbon dating comes into its own. A large series of dates is now available to show that the Early Neolithic of Britain began some centuries before 3000 BC. This is where the Cadbury pottery and flints should belong. But here a second snag in the method appears. The basic assumption has just been stated: 'that the rate of decay is constant'. Here we archaeologists would do well to remind ourselves that the physicists did not develop C-14 dating for our benefit – they wanted to use datable archaeological material to test their theories about the decay of radio-carbon. And external checks have now shown that the rate of decay has not been constant. Something is seriously amiss with the method, and in the Early Neolithic in particular C-14 dates may be as much as eight hundred years too late. So the beginning of the phase in Britain is, on current thinking, to be dated back before 4000 BC.[25] Let us not think, however, that the oracle has spoken finally.

Bearing all this in mind, we can now look at the C-14 dates from Cadbury itself. First of all, we have dated material from the ritual pit which has already been described, P154. A red-deer antler gave the date 2510 $\pm$ 120 BC; in other words, there is a 2:1 chance that the date lies in the bracket 2630–2390 BC. Some burnt hazel nut shells were also examined, and for them the bracket is 2870–2640. From the statistical point of view these dates are not really distinguishable. Applying the corrections which seem to be appropriate at the time of writing, we may probably date pit P154, and the pottery, flints and so on which it contained, to the period 3600–3400 BC. This agrees well with radio-carbon dates for comparable pottery from other southern English sites. It places Cadbury in a mature phase of the Early Neolithic.

The Late Neolithic and earlier Bronze Age

The Early Neolithic settlement established no long-term occupation on the hill. The early third millennium B C is a blank; but towards its mid-point comes another Neolithic phase, even more shadowy than the first. Among the worked flints found in 1966 were a few triangular flakes with an oblique cutting edge. These are a form of arrow-head, derived ultimately from the chisel-ended or *tranchet* arrow-heads of ancient hunting peoples, and known therefore as '*petit-tranchet* derivatives'. At first sight, the form does not suggest a missile point, and this is probably why none had been recorded in the surface collections from Cadbury. They are nonetheless quite characteristic of the Late Neolithic in the centuries around 2500 B C. Had they been lost in the course of hunting over pasture-land or scrub, or would we find contemporary pottery and traces of settlement? These questions were finally answered in 1969, when we discovered a large part of a Late Neolithic bowl of the Rinyo-Clacton or 'grooved-ware' style. Beside it, a stake-hole hinted at some kind of flimsy building. But as the discovery was made well below the base of the earliest rampart in Cutting A, and some fifteen feet below the modern ground surface, we were not able to examine the Late Neolithic phase any further. The earlier phases of a settlement must often remain unexplored simply because they are the most deeply buried.

Plate 22; *Fig. 14*

Plate 21

After the Late Neolithic, Cadbury was again deserted. The only finds are a barbed-and-tanged flint arrow-head which denotes hunting on the hill some time before 2000 B C; and an early form of cast bronze axe, characteristic of the Early Bronze Age around the beginning of the second millennium. The next event is a rather curious radio-carbon date of 925 ±90 B C, implying a true date which probably lies in the twelfth century B C. This came from ox-bones which had been found in the lowest twelve inches of the red-clay filling of the supposed Neolithic ditch, K618. The implication was that the ditch had been standing open in the twelfth century B C, so it could not possibly have been dug two millennia earlier. It is equally clear that the red clay and the bones it contained were deposited in the ditch around this time. When the first Iron Age rampart was built, K618 was already silted up to the general slope of the ground, and a considerable depth of humus had formed over it.

In other words, it is impossible to regard K618 as the precursor of the Iron Age defences. We only have evidence for it around 0.3 per cent of the perimeter. Moreover, the radio-carbon date for its infilling is substantially earlier than the archaeological date of the next phase of occupation.

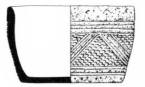

14 Restored Late Neolithic bowl with Rinyo-Clacton or grooved-ware ornament. Depth 4½ ins

113

In brief, K618 is an isolated feature which has no significant place in the history of Cadbury as we understand it at present.

The beginnings of settled life

Fig. 15

The clearest sign of renewed activity on the hill takes us into an advanced stage of the Late Bronze Age, in the years after 800 BC. The evidence is provided by metal objects, both gold and bronze, which were found scattered through the topsoil. The most spectacular was half a gold bracelet in the form of a penannular strip of gold, with a half-round section, and outwardly flattened terminals. Bracelets of this 'Covesea' type, made rarely of gold and more commonly of bronze, are known chiefly from north-eastern England and east Scotland, though related types do occur widely throughout the British Isles.[26] The Covesea bracelets of the north-east are regarded as a foreign element, introduced to the area by trade or by the movement of peoples in the eighth century. If this is true of the Cadbury example too, then it anticipates other foreign influences which we shall see shortly. Certainly the mere fact that the bracelet is of gold reflects a degree of wealth in the Late Bronze Age community.

15 *Gold bracelet of Covesea type, restored. Diameter 4¼ ins*

The humbler bronzes, on the other hand, all appear to be local, or at least to be the products of Irish or British bronzesmiths. They include complete and fragmentary spearheads; knives with a hollow socket to take a bone or wooden handle; and part of a strengthening plate from the base of a large bucket or pail of sheet bronze. Such miscellaneous collections of bronze, consisting partly of scrap and broken objects, partly of finished products, are very common in the Late Bronze Age. It is assumed that the scrap had been collected by travelling bronzesmiths who intended to melt it down to make new knives, axes and so on. These hoards of bronzes are frequently found buried in such a way as to suggest that their original owner had hidden them for safety, and had not returned to recover them. The simplest explanation of the Cadbury bronzes, and of the fragmentary Covesea bracelet too, is that they come from such a hoard, which had been buried at no great depth, and subsequently had been disturbed and scattered by ploughing. If this explanation were the whole story, we would have no need to think of an actual Late Bronze Age settlement at Cadbury.

Fig. 16

In addition to the metal objects, however, we found some distinctive pottery vessels which could probably be attributed to the same period. I use the word 'attributed' to show that here we are in the realms of inference, rather than of established fact. The reason for this is that, although pottery characteristic of the Early and Middle Bronze Age is known from many sites in southern England, pottery of the Late Bronze Age has been recognized only very rarely. That from Cadbury consists principally of large storage jars, in a fabric which is heavily filled with calcite grits. The shapes are simple bowls, barrels and pails. Some of these jars are very thin-walled for their size, and are smoothly finished, but the majority have rough exteriors, with vertical fluting where the potter has drawn his fingers down the outside, pulling the clay out to a splayed base. Only one vessel has any ornament: a row of dimples made by pinching the soft clay between finger and thumb.

In very broad terms, the date of this pottery is indicated by the discovery of a characteristic bowl in Trench A above the Rinyo-Clacton bowl of the Late Neolithic but below the earliest of the Iron Age ramparts. To establish its date more closely, we must compare it with the pottery of other periods. The shape of the vessels and their fabric both show conclusively that they do not belong in the Iron Age. On the other hand, some of the shapes are at least reminiscent of the 'Deverel-Rimbury' style which is characteristic of the Middle Bronze Age in southern England. One fragment may actually come from a Deverel-Rimbury bucket-urn, and another from a Deverel-Rimbury globular urn. But as a group, the Cadbury pottery cannot be assigned to the Deverel-Rimbury culture, in which the vessels are lavishly decorated with finger-pinched and finger-impressed ornament; this, as we have seen, is very rare at Cadbury. One possible hypothesis is that the pottery we attribute to the Late Bronze Age represents a degeneration from the classic Deverel-Rimbury style. In other words, between the twelfth century BC when the classic style flourishes, and the eighth or seventh century – the date suggested by the Cadbury metalwork – the forms of vessels had changed relatively little, but the finger-ornament had been abandoned.

An alternative hypothesis derives inspiration from the gold Covesea bracelet. In their main area of distribution, north-east Britain, Covesea bracelets are associated with pottery which does not fit into the local development of pottery styles. In other words, this pottery is probably intrusive, as the bracelets certainly are. While it cannot be compared in detail with that from Cadbury, it certainly includes large, very simple jars which seem to reflect similar technical and aesthetic standards. Do the gold bracelet and the Late Bronze Age pottery from Cadbury represent a southern wave of the same tide of invasion as the Covesea bracelets and associated pottery denote in the north-east? If this could be established, it would be an event of great importance, for it would mark the beginnings of what was soon to

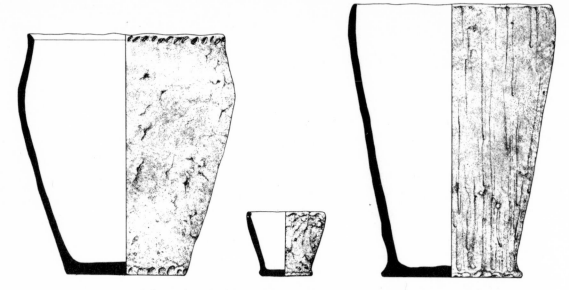

16 Restored vessels of the Late Bronze Age. The jar with finger-pinched ornament below the rim is the one found in the oven-pit; see Plates 24, 25. The larger jar is 13 ¼ ins high

become a flood of Celtic invasions from the continent. But this hypothesis is not pressed here, simply because at present we do not know enough about the development of the Deverel-Rimbury style or about Late Bronze Age pottery from other sites to be able to judge between the alternatives.

Whatever the ultimate implication of this Late Bronze Age pottery, its occurrence at Cadbury certainly argues for permanent occupation of the hill-top. There is also definite evidence to show that the occupation was domestic in character. Along with the pottery were clay loom-weights, for tensioning the warp threads of a vertical loom. Their cylindrical shape can be paralleled at other Bronze Age villages. Some of the pottery occurred in rock-cut pits, which had been dug originally to store grain or other food, and had later been filled in with rubbish. One pit, however, had been an oven, not a larder. A pot, probably containing stew, had been placed in the pit, and hot ashes had then been packed around it until the meal was cooked. Unfortunately for some Bronze Age housewife, on one occasion the upper third of the pot had split away, leaving the base, and a ruined meal, still in the pit.

Although we can establish that people were living permanently on the Cadbury hill during the eighth and seventh centuries B C, we can say nothing at present about the character of their houses. It used to be thought that Late Bronze Age houses were quite small circular structures. On these grounds some shallow gullies on Site F, with arcs of about seven foot radius, were attributed to this period. But our whole concept of Bronze Age houses has

Plates 24, 25

Fig. 16

Fig. 8, B, C

recently been challenged, and there is now no reason why these gullies should indicate houses of the seventh century BC rather than the early first century AD.[27] It is possible that a more refined study of the distribution of Bronze Age finds, and especially of the pits and ovens, may eventually make it possible to point to the contemporary houses. In the present state of Cadbury studies, the most we can say is that the characteristic pottery is concentrated in a small area of the summit plateau. This restricted distribution suggests that the settlement itself was no more than a hamlet of three or four houses, occupied by a handful of families.

What is certain is that the hamlet was not fortified. There is no evidence, whether from air-photography, geophysical survey, or excavation, that it was ever enclosed by a defensive stockade. And it is quite certain that the earliest rampart and ditch of the hillfort are works of later centuries altogether. If their purpose was not defence, why did Late Bronze Age men choose to live on the top of a hill? The answer probably lies in a climatic deterioration, which brought colder and wetter weather to the British Isles in the first millennium BC. This would have forced men to forsake the lowlands of Somerset and seek better drained lands, both for farming and for habitation, on the surrounding hills. At Cadbury their first act was to burn off the scrub and timber which had grown up since the days of the Neolithic farmers. The Bronze Age vessel from Site A lay in a level black with the charcoal from this burning. From what we know of other Bronze Age settlements the land immediately around the village would then have been tilled. On the other hand, the depth of the humus which had been preserved under the earliest rampart shows that for decades or even centuries before the rampart was built the margins of the hill-top had not been cultivated. This outlying area, and the actual hill-slopes, were doubtless used for grazing cattle and sheep.

The fact that this hill-top settlement was undefended has wider implications which deserve a brief discussion. It has usually been considered in the past that the construction of hillforts in southern Britain did not begin before the Iron Age: the earliest ones may have been built in the fifth century BC, but the majority were works of the third century or later. Recently, however, some doubts have been cast on this chronology by the recognition that hillforts were being built well before the fifth century on the continent, and probably – on the evidence of radio-carbon dating – in Scotland and Wales as well.[28] Since metalwork of the Late Bronze Age has occasionally been found in other hillforts, such as Traprain Law in eastern Scotland, the question arose whether, in default of C-14 dates, the metalwork proved a

Bronze Age date for the foundation of these forts too. The Cadbury evidence shows that this need not necessarily be the case. Unless Bronze Age metal-work is found in a definite relationship with the ramparts, its presence in a hillfort may be purely coincidental.

The beginning of the Iron Age

Sometime in the late seventh or sixth century BC the Cadbury hamlet passed from a Late Bronze to an Iron Age cultural phase. It must be stressed at once that this transition is a shadowy one not merely at Cadbury but in British archaeology as a whole, and consequently there has been a great deal of discussion and even controversy about its character. Part of this has tended to be an arid debate about terminology. If, for instance, a site produces pottery which is clearly ancestral to regular Iron Age forms, but without associated iron tools and weapons, can it legitimately be called Iron Age? Or again, if a settlement has normal Late Bronze Age implements, but untypical pottery, is it still to be classed as Bronze Age? These terminological problems are best left in the hands of the pedants who delight in them.

There are, however, deeper issues involved as well. They turn essentially on the question whether it was immigrants or natives who played the major part in fashioning the cultures of the British Iron Age. Related to this is the question when the Celtic language – the speech of the ancient Britons, the ancestor of modern Gaelic, Cornish and Welsh – was introduced from western Europe to these islands, and whether it was brought by large-scale folk-migration or by small groups of warrior chiefs. It is quite certain that the use of iron weapons and tools, and the craft of smelting and forging iron, were introduced from the area of the Hallstatt culture – the first iron-using culture of western and west-central Europe. It is equally certain that when the inhabitants of the Hallstatt area first appeared in historical records, they were Celtic peoples. Was the use of iron brought to Britain, along with Celtic speech and other aspects of Celtic culture, by a mass-movement of land-hungry peasants; by noble warriors with attendant blacksmiths; or simply by a few enterprising traders and craftsmen?

Previous discussions of the strength of the immigrant elements in the Iron Age, and of the relative roles of natives and invaders, have concentrated on two aspects of culture: houses and pottery. It has been claimed that whereas the houses of Hallstatt Europe were invariably rectangular, those of Iron Age Britain were equally invariably circular. Since the houses of the British Bronze Age were also circular, the Iron Age round-house must reflect the

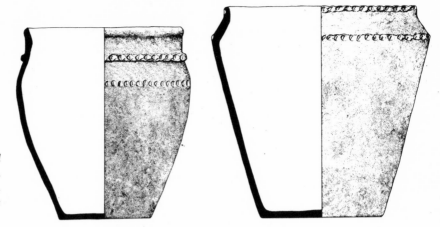

17 Restored jars of the Initial and Early Iron Age phases, with finger-tip ornament. The larger jar is 11¼ ins high

continuity of native traditions. Secondly, the earliest pottery of the British Iron Age is frequently decorated with finger-tip or finger-nail impressions. Similar ornament is very common in the Bronze Age too, especially on Deverel-Rimbury pottery. Granted that the shapes of the vessels differ from the earlier period to the later, and the ornament is differently arranged, nevertheless it seemed likely that the Bronze Age ornament was ancestral to that of the Iron Age. Here, then, was another element of native continuity.

At this point, the reader who is not already familiar with this debate, or already committed to a particular position in it, should be warned that neither of the generalizations of the previous paragraph will stand up to critical examination. This warning will be amplified with concrete examples in a moment; but another warning is also necessary. Much of the debate has been conducted so far in terms of old, and often unreliable, excavations and discoveries. What is now needed is close and critical attention to the observable course of events on individual sites where both Bronze and Iron Age material is present. What follows is an account of developments at Cadbury Castle, which claims validity for this site alone.

I begin with the pottery. The whole sequence of pottery in the Iron Age at Cadbury can be divided into five fairly well-defined phases. Each of these can be paralleled on other British Iron Age sites, but the full sequence is not at present known anywhere else. The five phases can conveniently be designated Initial, Early, Middle, Late and Ultimate. At present we are concerned only with the Initial pottery. There is not a lot of this, but its characteristics are clear. It consists of large jars or bowls with fairly pronounced shoulders. Ornament is limited to finger-tip impressions on the shoulder, on the rim, and also, most characteristic of all, on an applied band or cordon of clay running round the neck of the vessel.

Fig.17

Fig. 16

Plate 23

Now we have already seen that finger-tip ornament is common on the Deverel-Rimbury pottery of the Bronze Age, and there too it occurs characteristically on applied bands or cordons. So at first sight our Initial pottery reflects native ceramic traditions. This view is, however, quite untenable. The finger-ornamented jars of the classic Deverel-Rimbury culture belong not to the centuries immediately before the Iron Age, but to the twelfth and eleventh centuries BC: in fact, to the Middle Bronze Age. And however long the style may have continued, we have already seen that Late Bronze Age pottery at Cadbury itself was almost entirely unornamented. Out of a good number of Late Bronze Age vessels, only one has finger-pinched ornament, and that is not on an applied cordon. In other words, our Initial pottery reflects not the continuity of native traits, but a complete break in the sequence.

On the other hand, when we look more widely, we find that finger-tip decoration on the rims and shoulders of jars, and even on neck-cordons, is very common in the Late Bronze Age of western Europe. This is especially true of the so-called Urnfield cultures of France. Moreover, jars with finger-impressed neck-cordons, quite comparable with the Cadbury examples, occur in the Hallstatt Iron Age of southern Germany.[29] There is a good case here that the Initial Iron Age pottery of Cadbury owes nothing at all to native forbears, but has been introduced from outside, most probably from the continent. When we consider that, throughout most of the Iron Age, pottery-making was essentially a domestic craft or cottage industry, it is evident that the appearance of new types of pottery implies the migration of the peasants who made and used it.

This conclusion leads us naturally to consider other exotic elements which occur in the Initial Iron Age at Cadbury. The most obvious are two bronze razors, one fragmentary and the other almost complete. These have parallels in the Hallstatt C phase of western Europe, especially in northern France, southern Germany and the Low Countries.[30] They are rare in Britain, but they occur at Staple Howe in Yorkshire along with finger-impressed neck-cordon pottery and some simple iron objects.[31] There is also a minor concentration in Somerset and Glamorgan, where the most important example, that from Llyn Fawr, was found with a Hallstatt C iron sword, a spearhead and a sickle, all betokening the beginning of the British Iron Age.[32] The Llyn Fawr sword was associated with Hallstatt C horse harness which had probably originated in southern Germany: the whole assemblage allows us to infer a noble Celtic warrior establishing himself in western Britain in the late seventh or sixth century. At Cadbury the trappings of aristocracy have not been found, though it is worth pointing out that Hallstatt C razors frequently occur in warrior graves in Burgundy. It is therefore possible that the peasantry, represented by the pottery, had migrated under the leadership of a military nobility.

So far we have examined only the exotic or immigrant elements of the Initial Iron Age, and we have therefore been led to emphasize its discontinuity with the Late Bronze Age. But when we consider the actual form of the settlement in each period, there is one remarkable similarity: these successive hill-top settlements were both undefended. The pottery sequence at Cadbury had already passed from the Initial into the Early phase before the earliest rampart was built. As in the Late Bronze Age, so in the Initial Iron Age there is no evidence to show that the hamlet or village was enclosed by a defensive stockade.

Indeed, apart from its pottery and bronzes and its absence of defences we know very little about the Initial Iron Age occupation. We have not recognized any storage pits or refuse pits containing material of the period. This may be because the use of such pits, common in the Late Bronze Age, had been given up, only to be resumed in later centuries. This is unlikely, and it is more probable that the contemporary pits lay outside the area of our excavations. This in turn might mean that, through the hazards of discovery, we had not located the main focus of Initial occupation. We could judge whether or not this was so if we could identify the contemporary houses, but we cannot do this with any certainty. It is true that on Site T we located *Fig. 11* a six-post rectangular house which was earlier than a spread of cobbling which itself had been laid down quite early in the Iron Age. But 'early' here is only a relative term. With seven hundred years of Iron Age occupation to account for, it would be rash to say that even the earliest of the six-post houses must belong to the Initial phase.

The mention of rectangular houses reintroduces one topic of the debate with which this section began. The claim that all Iron Age continental houses were rectangular has always appeared to be a gross over-simplification. Greek travellers, for instance, refer to the dome-like dwellings of the Celtic peoples of northern France. We can now see that the parallel generalization, that all British Iron Age houses were circular, is equally untrue. Scattered through early excavation reports are occasional examples of rectangular houses, to which the supporters of the generalization turned a blind eye. But they can less easily ignore the evidence of recent excavations, carried out at the highest level of competence.[33] Both four- and six-post rectangular buildings are now widely known from Iron Age sites through-

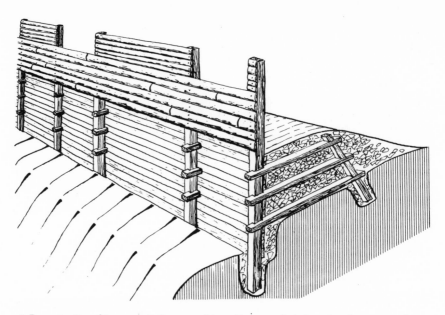

18 Reconstruction of Rampart A. For some of the evidence on which this is based, see Fig. 7, features 524, 541, 546, 694

out southern England. Much more research is needed, however, both in Britain and on the continent, before we can assert that such buildings represent an intrusive element in the British Iron Age. At Cadbury, the case for immigration rests, as we have seen, on the pottery and the bronzes.

The first defences

Plates 11, 23

Fig. 17

A second period of continental influence, the Hallstatt D phase, is represented at Cadbury by several very distinctive pins made of bent wire, the so-called 'swan's neck' pins. On the continent, a date in the fifth century BC would be appropriate for these. In the Cadbury Iron Age sequence, they belong in the second phase, the Early Iron Age. The pottery is now dominated by coarse jars and large bowls with a well-marked shoulder. There is often finger-tip ornament on the shoulder itself, but the neck-cordon has vanished. Finer bowls with angular sides ornamented with faintly incised diagonal lines are less common. The fine bowls may represent a further continental influence, but the coarser vessels could be an insular development from the Initial jars.

By the Hallstatt D phase, fortifications were proliferating in Celtic Europe; and this is the date too of the first defence at Cadbury. Some of

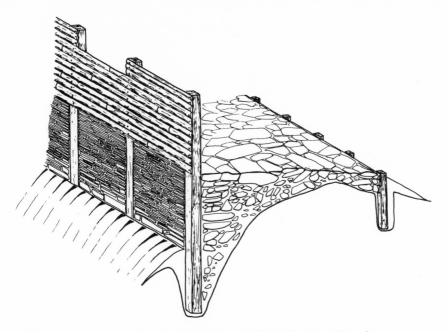

19 Reconstruction of Rampart B. For the evidence on which this is based, see Fig. 7, features 522, 530, 530 B, 693. Oblique projection

the continental Hallstatt forts appear to be the strongholds of princes, whose rich burials are found in the neighbourhood.[34] But no comparable burials have been found in Britain, and it is quite uncertain whether the stimulus to fort-building came from a warrior aristocracy, or from peasant communities who found themselves pressed by other groups of land-hungry farmers. The size of the first Cadbury fort, about twenty acres, favours the idea that it was built for a large but lowly social unit, not as a warrior-chief's private defence. The actual evidence for the date of the first rampart is provided by a few sherds of pottery: in Cutting D, a rim from a neck-cordon jar was certainly found beneath it, while in Cut A vessels of both the Initial and Early phases probably came from below the rampart.

The structure of the first defence, Rampart A, was fully explored in Cutting D. The body of the rampart was a bank of clay and small rubble or gravel. At the front of this was a row of holes which had held posts up to six inches across. Immediately behind the posts, a ledge had been cut in the ground, obviously to seat a horizontal timber. From this we can infer that the upright posts had been backed by horizontal shoring, giving an almost vertical face to the rampart. Five feet behind the front posts was a second row, and there was slight evidence that the two rows had been tied together by transverse horizontal beams. Rampart A was thus a timber

Plate 30

Figs. 7, 18

123

VI   The south-west gate in 1970. The visible walling is that of the Ultimate Iron Age gate. In the passage-way, the massacre level is being explored.

VII   The south-eastern defences seen from the air.

VIII, IX   Front and back views of a Celtic bronze pendant embellished with white paste or coral studs. Diameter 1 ½ ins.

X   Examples of inlaid metal-work. A link from a Roman harness-set, in bronze inlaid with silver, length 2 ¾ ins. Half of an iron neck-ring, inlaid with brass, found in the massacre level at the south-west gate. Note the tang which engages in a socket in the other half of the ring.

XI   Silver ring or buckle with Germanic animal ornament of the sixth century AD, found beneath the relaid road surface of the Arthurian gate. Tinned bronze disk ornamented with a repoussé horse in a style similar to that of the Celtic coins.

XII   Bronze plaque, ornamented with a human or divine face in a mixed Celtic and romanizing style. Found face downwards in the ruins of the Ultimate Iron Age guard-chamber at the south-west gate. Height 5 ¼ins.

XIII   Imported pottery of the late fifth and early sixth centuries. Top row: rim and body sherds from Class A bowls – note the cross-stamp on the right (compare *Fig. 27*). Middle rows: body sherds, and a handle fragment, from wine-jars of Class Bi. Bottom row: two body sherds from Class Bii wine-jars; sherd from a Class Biv wine-jar; rim from a Class D bowl (compare *Fig. 27*).

XIV   Gilt-bronze button brooch of Pagan Saxon type, ornamented with a helmeted head. Diameter ⅔ in.

XV   Late Saxon pottery: an unusual ornamented piece, and characteristic examples of the heavily-gritted fabrics. The largest sherd is 3 ½ ins across.

VI

VII

VIII   IX

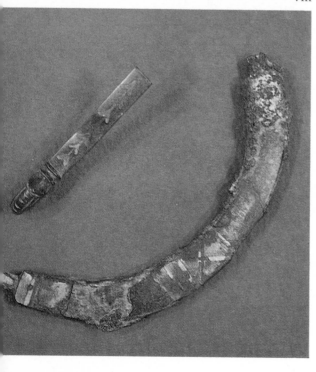

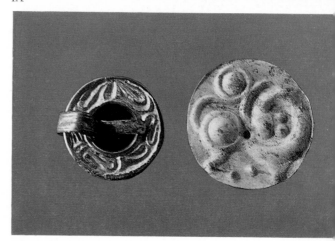

XI

X

XIII

XIV   XV

structure, filled in with clay and rubble. We do not know how the timber-work was fastened together, but continental evidence shows that the Celts were already masters of the techniques of carpentry jointing.

In front of the front timbers, and probably separated from them by a more or less level ledge or berm, was a rock-cut ditch. The bank material had been quarried from the ditch, and from its character we can infer that the ditch was not very deep; certainly it had not penetrated through the topmost weathered levels into really solid rock. This arrangement of bank, timber wall, berm and ditch comprised the whole of the first defensive scheme. The line of the rampart was set at the point where the relatively gentle slopes of the upper part of the hill dropped steeply away: it was sited to take the maximum advantage of the natural strength of the hill. Because of the shape of the hill, with its pronounced axial ridge, the trace of the rampart does not follow a contour line, as Iron Age ramparts often do. Instead, it climbs about fifty feet over the ridge at either end.

Fig. 21

Fig. 4

The circuit of the bank was a little over twelve hundred yards. From this fact, something of the effort required to build Rampart A may be calculated. About nine hundred stout posts would have been needed for the front of the bank, together with a run of at least seventy thousand feet of planking for the shoring and breastwork. The rear posts and cross ties would have added yet more. So there was a major operation involved in cutting and dressing the timber, before any defences could be assembled. Compared with this side of the work the digging of the ditch and throwing up of the bank was a simple, unskilled job. It is quite evident that considerable communal effort and a strong organization were both involved. Unfortunately, in these remote times we can have no real evidence as to how the necessary labour services were exacted and organized; but we may believe that the motives which impelled men to such efforts were very powerful.

We do not know how long Rampart A remained in existence. The front posts would eventually have rotted at ground level, but there is no convincing evidence to show how soon this would have happened. In Cut D there was no sign that timbers had ever been renewed. On the other hand, there are hints that the first rampart was already derelict and grassed over before Rampart B was erected on top of its ruins. The pottery which is contemporary with the building of the second rampart is transitional between the Early and Middle phases in the Cadbury sequence.

Rampart B was altogether a more substantial affair. For a start, the ditch was now dug down into very solid rock, which on the south side of the hill provided great blocks and slabs of Inferior Oolitic limestone for the body of

Figs. 7, 19

Plates 29, 30

the bank. These slabs were roughly laid to give a fairly level top to the bank, in fact a crude rampart walk. At the front there was a row of posts which were considerably stouter than those of Rampart A, but this time they did not support timber shoring. Instead, the core of the bank was masked by a skin of Lias limestone slabs, imported from some miles away. The appearance of this rampart must have been striking, but structurally-speaking it was not very sound. The timber uprights contributed weakness rather than strength to the wall face. The facing itself was not keyed back into the core, so that from the start it must have tended to slip. Finally the Lias, which originally had split into regular slabs very convenient for building, then continued to split into thinner and smaller pieces. Rampart B was evidently a showy rather than a sound defensive work.

Plate 32

It is from this phase that we have our first evidence for the Iron Age gate arrangements. I have already explained that the progressive wearing down of the entrance passage had left the earlier guard-chambers standing above the level of the ultimate road-way. A small area of the highest guard-chamber floor had survived the erosion of the road and the cutting down of subsequent guard-chambers. It was bounded by a curving rock-cut trench, in which the ghost of a plank wall could still be discerned. A doorway, flanked by sturdy posts, opened not into the passage-way, but into the interior of the fort. The implication of this is that the guardroom was set not beside the passage but at its inner end, backing onto the rampart. Patches of burned clay and scatters of charcoal from hearths show that the guard-chamber had been lived in, and a series of occupation-floors had accumulated as a result. The uppermost of these contained a quantity of pottery which can be placed very firmly in the Middle Iron Age. That period, and the succeeding Late Iron Age, are the subject of the next chapter.

VI The Iron Age town

In the last chapter, we saw the occupation of Cadbury grow from an un-fortified hamlet of the Late Bronze Age to a defended village of peasant farmers in the Early Iron Age. The subsequent Middle and Late phases of the Iron Age saw a great intensification and diversification of human activity on the hill-top. In the archaeological record this is reflected by a much greater range of finds, and these in vastly greater quantities. Within the defences, storage pits and timber round-houses proliferated. By this stage, the settlement can no longer be considered as a village, still less as a hamlet. In terms of the density of population implied by the number of houses, it is reasonable to describe it as a town. This would also agree with the development of both industry and commerce. This chapter, then, is devoted to the details of the evidence on which these broad statements are based.

Developments in pottery

In terms of pottery and other finds, the Middle Iron Age at Cadbury was extremely dull. As the pottery was washed and given a preliminary sorting on the site, we tended to place in the 'Middle' phase anything which lacked the well defined characteristics of the other phases in our sequence. In other words, the Middle Iron Age appeared as a rag-bag for nondescript material. But when the excavations were over, as we studied the groups of finds *Fig. 20* associated together in refuse pits, or in stratified deposits in the ramparts, it became clear that Middle Iron Age pottery had a character of its own, even if it had to be defined in negative terms. It appeared to have developed out of the Early pottery by a process of simplification, and above all by the abandonment of even the most rudimentary type of decoration, the row of finger impressions. The most characteristic form was a small to medium-sized jar or bowl with an S-shaped profile. The clay was heavily backed with particles of fossil shell obtained from the local Jurassic limestone. The finish

20 *Restored vessels of the Middle and Late Iron Age phases. A common type of Middle jar; a saucepan pot; a large storage jar; a bowl with incised decoration; and a simple bead-rim bowl. The large jar is 12 ½ ins high*

Fig. 20

of vessels was generally poor, but there was a tendency to smooth or even burnish the exterior.

By contrast with these simple vessels, the pottery of the Late phase exhibits a wide range of form and decoration. Indeed, when the analysis is completed, it will probably reveal that there are several sub-phases, and that numerous outside influences had affected the development of Late pottery at Cadbury. A continuing tradition is represented by large, rather coarse storage jars, which have their roots in the Initial and Early phases. Innovation, on the other hand, is seen in smaller jars, with a simple curved profile, which are normally finished with a highly burnished exterior. These jars frequently have a distinctive 'beaded' rim, and variations of this rim are then found on both bowls and jars over a period of some centuries. Another well-marked form is a deep straight-sided bowl, known as a 'sauce-pan pot', though it is doubtful whether it could have been used on an open fire.

But the most important development is in ornament. Any group of Late pottery will contain, alongside a majority of undecorated sherds, a few which have a distinctive ornament of incised lines or grooves, or more rarely of grooves and pits. Rows of triangles, picked out with either diagonal or criss-cross hatching, form one common motif, but scrolls, waves and other curvilinear designs are equally important. Sometimes the curves are compass drawn. At their best, the designs are based on those of contemporary Celtic metalwork, and it is certain that continental artistic influences derived from the La Tène art-style are at work. It is also clear that Cadbury stands towards the eastern boundary of an aesthetic province which includes the whole of south-western Britain. Within this province, the Somerset lake-villages of Glastonbury and Meare were important manufacturing centres, as well as leaders in design. The most sophisticated Late vessels at Cadbury had probably been traded from Glastonbury, though the majority of the pottery had been made on the spot, often to disgustingly debased designs.

The close dating of these developments in pottery awaits a great deal of research and publication throughout the south-west. Very tentatively, we might suggest that the Late style was becoming established about 200 B C. It may have continued to the end of the pre-Christian era, though new influences appeared by the middle of the first century B C. The Middle phase at Cadbury might cover the fourth and third centuries. But the lay reader – and the archaeological pedant – should be warned that in this period, dates are nothing more than ideas in the mind of another archaeologist.

Developments in defence

It is evident from the rampart cuttings – especially A, D and K – that Bank 1 was reconstructed several times during the Middle and Late Iron Age. It is difficult to be more precise than this, because ramparts have been lost by collapse and erosion on the steep slopes, or have been mutilated by later defence-building. There is evidence in Trench D for rear-walls or revetments to sentry walks, but no trace at all of front revetments or facing walls. This may mean simply that the revetments of Ramparts C and D have collapsed downhill. On the other hand, it could mean that Cadbury, like contemporary Maiden Castle, had adopted the so-called 'glacis-fronted' rampart, with a long even slope from the bottom of the ditch to the crest of the bank: an ideal killing ground. But given the major geological difference between Maiden Castle on chalk and Cadbury on a limestone which provides good building slabs, this is unlikely.

It was during the Late period that the outer defences of Cadbury were built. This can be asserted partly by comparison with other southern English hillforts, partly on internal evidence. Bank 4 had been constructed, had grassed over, and had then been refurbished by the end of the Iron Age. If we assign the refurbishing to the Ultimate phase, perhaps in the generation before the Roman Conquest, then the original Bank 4 was built in the Late Iron Age. And a massive work it was, with a basal width of over twenty feet,

Fig. 7

Plates 15, 28

Fig. 21

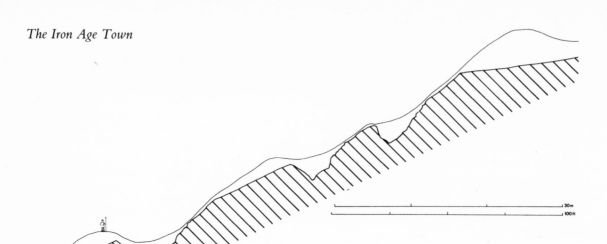

21 Outline profile of the Iron Age ditches as revealed by the excavation of Site D

and a height of twelve feet or so above an internal rock-cut ditch. The inner, or scarp, slope of that ditch rose at an angle of almost fifty degrees for a slope distance of twenty feet, before easing off to a mere thirty-five degrees towards Bank 3. This seems to have been a relatively feeble obstacle, but behind it was Ditch 2, with a scarp which in places rose at nearly eighty degrees – a minor rock-climbing problem. The main objective of the multiple defences at Cadbury was evidently to improve on nature by producing even steeper scarp slopes. The banks were little more than a by-product of throwing downhill the rubble produced by scarping and ditching.

Plate 35

There is some evidence for the lay-out of the south-west gateway in the Late Iron Age. Its main feature was a pair of oval guard-chambers, opening directly into the passage-way. To cope with the developing hollow-way, the guard-chamber floors had been sunk into the solid rock, and the walls were then carried up in dry stonework. Pairs of massive post-pits marked the doorways from the chambers to the passage, and linked up with equally massive pits along the roadway itself. These had held posts for the main gates, and may also have supported a sentry-walk or fighting platform over the entrance. By comparing the Cadbury remains with other paired guard-chamber lay-outs, we can speculate that there may have been as many as four double-leaved gates set one behind another along the passage-way: clearly a very formidable defensive scheme.[35] There is some shadowy evidence that the lay-out of the Middle period gate was similar to this, but the left-hand guard-chamber has almost completely vanished as a result of erosion.

The Iron Age town

Within the defences, the most obvious feature of the Iron Age town was the circular houses, which we infer from rock-cut trenches or from the dark stains of stake-holes. The complete plan of a stake-built house and part of another were uncovered on Site B, where the yellow sandstone revealed the pattern of stake-holes particularly clearly. One was about thirty, and the other about thirty-five feet in diameter with floor areas respectively of seven hundred and one thousand square feet. For the smaller house, a level emplacement had been prepared by cutting into the sloping hillside to a depth of three feet or so. A narrow trench was then dug to take the base of the wall, and stakes were driven into the soft bedrock along its line. The stakes themselves were two to four inches in diameter, and were set between six and twelve inches apart. In and out of these uprights horizontal withies would be woven, to make a rigid structure like a large basket. By the time that the wattle had been plastered with a daub of clay and cow-dung, and a thatch roof had been added, a substantial house would have been in existence.

In the case of the rock-cut trenches of the summit plateau, the structural interpretation is less certain. Some of the ring-trenches were both narrow and shallow, and it is very probable that these had held wattle walls of the kind which were so clear on Site B. But most of those which we uncovered were from two to five feet wide and up to three feet deep. Two were certainly complete rings, but two others were penannular, one of them (on Site T) having a gap of about thirteen feet between the ditch ends. This seems much too wide for a door-way, and it is therefore unlikely in this case that the trench had held the house-wall: it was probably a drainage gully, taking the water from the eaves. On the other hand, a house in the middle of Site P apparently had post-holes for a porch outside the ditch, so here the ditch must have held the wall itself. There is indeed good evidence that this was in the form of split logs or planks placed side by side. But the kind of inference which the archaeologist normally expects to make from soil stains, position of packing stones and so on was only rarely possible at Cadbury, where the ring-ditches usually contained an undifferentiated fill of gravelly soil.[36]

But if evidence for the superstructure of these buildings has escaped us in most cases, there are still useful facts to be established about them. For a start: it was customary for a house to be rebuilt several times on the same spot, perhaps with a very slight shift of its centre or of part of its wall line. We can infer this from multiple arcs of stake-holes on Site B, or clear signs

Fig. 10

Plates 53, 69

Plates 40, 44, 45

Plates 45, IV, V
Fig. 11

of re-cutting in the profiles of the ring-ditches on Sites E F G, P and T. This suggests continuity of occupation or ownership over a long period. Secondly, the houses are mostly in the same size range, around thirty to forty feet in diameter, seven to twelve hundred square feet in area. This marks them off on the one hand from the much smaller houses which have normally been found in hillforts, and on the other from the distinctly larger Iron Age houses which have been discovered outside true hillforts.[37] Size must reflect an equation between the number of inhabitants per hut and the degree of comfort; and the comfort which the inhabitants expected may be related to their social status. I shall have more to say about status later, but on the matter of numbers we might guess that each house was occupied by ten to twenty persons, and perhaps some livestock.[38]

Figs. 6, 8

Apart from the houses, the most obvious feature of Iron Age Cadbury is the rock-cut pits, which appear so strongly on the air-photographs and in the geophysical survey. Excavation showed that these varied in shape, diameter and depth; but the tendency was for them to be as cylindrical as local rock conditions would allow. Exceptionally they might be up to eight or even ten feet across, and six feet deep, but a good average would be six feet in diameter and four feet deep. The main function of the pits was probably to store grain, either in sacks and baskets, or poured loose into the pit, which would then have been covered with a basketry lid and made watertight with a clay seal. A normal Cadbury pit might have held about eighty bushels of threshed grain (but considerably less if the grain was stored in the husk). This might have been sufficient to feed a family of eight – men, women and children – for a year; so perhaps the occupants of a round-house would have needed two grain pits.[39]

In course of time, we believe, these grain stores became sour, and an attempt was made to cleanse them by burning straw and brushwood in the bottom. Many of the Cadbury pits had their sides fire-reddened in this way. But eventually, no amount of burning was of any use, and the pits had to be abandoned. They were then filled in, partly with stone dug from new pits which were to replace them, partly with domestic refuse. Consequently, many of the pits are a rich source for pottery, and more rarely objects of bone and metal. But this explanation will not fit all the pits which we observed. Some contained one or more animal skulls placed in such positions that it was difficult to believe that they had been shot in as rubbish. All the skulls, of horses and cattle, were set the right way up, and one was even laid on a bed of stones. In fact, they gave every impression of having been deliberately buried as part of some ritual. A ritual purpose also seems likely for

Plates 42, 54

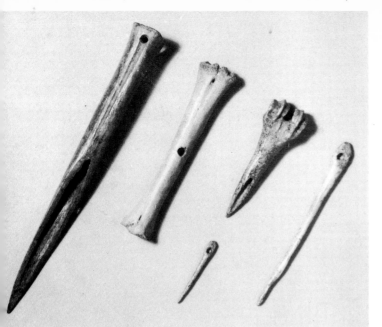

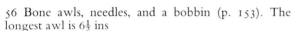

56 Bone awls, needles, and a bobbin (p. 153). The longest awl is 6½ ins

57 Obverse and reverse of three Celtic coins. The re- > verse is based on a horse-and-chariot design, while the obverse bears an ear of barley or the head of Apollo (*Fig. 25*). The top coin is the gold stater of Antethos of the Dobunnic tribe; the others are Durotrigian issues (pp. 166–7)

58 Bone and antler weaving-combs or skin-scrapers, a very characteristic domestic implement throughout the British Iron Age (p. 153). The right-hand scraper is 5 ins long

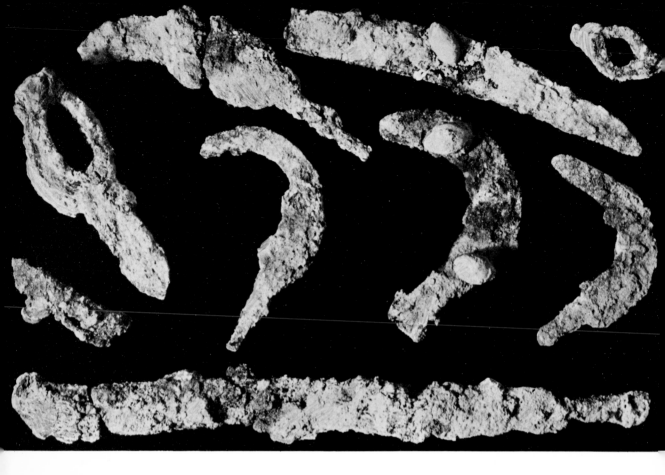

59, 60 Hoard of iron objects buried in the back of Bank 1 in a late phase of the Iron Age (pp. 153–4): knife; saw (see also Plate 61); binding or ferrule; axe; three sickles (see Plate 61); two knives corroded together; currency bar. The axe and part of the currency bar are seen below after conservation. Clay sling-bullets are rusted on to the saw and one of the sickles. The overall length of the currency bar is 21 ins

61, 62 Domestic and craft implements of iron: a saw with two rivets to fasten the wooden handle; wool-shears; two sickles with sockets for the handle; three knives. The saw is 12¾ ins long, the largest knife is 7¾ ins (pp. 153–4)

63 Iron weapons: a shield boss and two spear-heads from the massacre level at the south-west gate (pp. 105, 170); two daggers from the weapon-burials on Site N (p. 84, see also Plate 47). The larger dagger is $15\frac{1}{4}$ ins long overall

64 Jointed neck-ring or torc of iron from the massacre level (p. 170); and part of a second inlaid with brass (see Plate X). About half actual size

65, 66 Bronze brooches of the dolphin, fiddle, thistle and penannular varieties, all except the fiddle from the massacre level at the south-west gate (pp. 105, 168–9, *Fig. 25*). All actual size. The brooch, *below*, has been opened out to show the intricacy of the spring attachment and mechanism; it is reproduced at about twice actual size

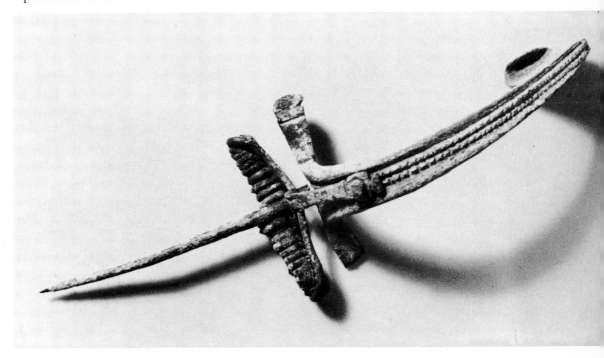

67 The first evidence of the massacre at the south-west gate; the leg of a young person, complete from hip to toe, found beneath the Arthurian-period roads (p. 105). With it can be seen an iron spear-head; a bronze bow brooch and a penannular brooch; and numerous fragments of pottery

68 The first stage in the area excavation of Site B in 1968 (pp. 73–4). Apart from slight remains of a capping of harder, paler limestone (top right), the bed-rock on Site B was a light yellow sandstone, which showed very clearly where wooden structures, including stakes of only two or three inches in diameter, had decayed (Plate 53). As soon as the bed-rock had been scraped clean, two parallel dark streaks appeared, marking the wall-trenches of a rectangular building. For the fuller development of the area, see Plate 69

69 The wider exploration of Site B in 1968 revealed both circular and rectangular buildings. In the foreground, the bed-rock is dipping into the 'Big Ditch' (*Fig. 10*, 31), first detected as a prominent crop-mark on the 1955 air-photographs (Plates 4 and 5), examined by means of a narrow trench in 1966 (p. 50), and subsequently identified as a hollow-way leading from the north-east gate up to the summit plateau (pp. 73–4). The edges of the Big Ditch were scalloped by emplacements levelled into the rock for building circular houses (*Fig. 10*, 25; Plate 53); the nearer two-metre pole lies on the floor of one of these emplacements. On the flat ground behind and to the left of the nearer pole are traces of an arc of stake-holes from a round house (*Fig. 10*, 24; pp. 84, 135). Subsequent to this, a group of rectangular buildings was erected; two of them can be seen here, and a third was traced to the north (right) in 1969 (*Fig. 10*, 30; p. 101). The regularity of layout of these buildings, the presence of a Roman field oven just across the hollow-way, and the discovery of much Roman military equipment on Site B (Plate 70–2) all combine to suggest that these are Roman military buildings (p. 172)

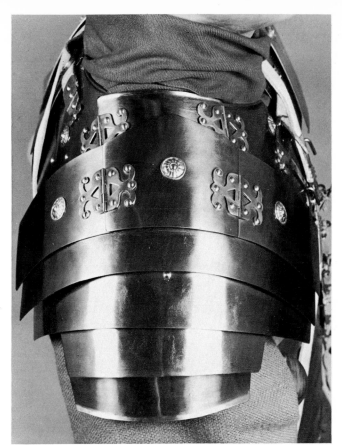

70–72 Items of Roman military equipment, all of bronze: one half of a hinge from a cuirass; a link from a harness set, inlaid with silver (see also Plate X); a mount from the 'apron' which protected the legionary's abdomen; a hinge from one of the straps used to fasten armour; and a binding strip from the edge of a legionary shield; all about 4/5ths actual size. The life-size model by H. Russell Robinson shows these various fittings (except for the harness-link) actually in use, with a close-up to clarify points of detail (pp. 51, 101, 172)

73 The latest structural phases of Bank 1 as revealed in Cutting D in 1967 (p. 67). The vertical two-metre pole stands against the inner face of the mortared perimeter wall of the Ethelredan *burh*. (For the outer face of this wall, as preserved on Site A, see Plate 86). A thin spread of mortar, spilt while the wall was being built, lies behind it; traces of this can be seen beneath the horizontal pole. The mortar spread was covered by an earthen bank, retained at the rear by the mortared wall seen behind the horizontal pole. This mortared rear-revetment was found nowhere else around the perimeter, suggesting that the construction of the *burh* defences had never been completed (p. 198). Immediately to the right of the Ethelredan rear-revetment, at a slightly higher level, are remains of a post-Ethelredan revetment of dry stonework, perhaps contemporary with the wall of big yellow stones at the south-west gate (p. 202, Plates 93, 94).

In the eastern (left-hand) half of the trench, Ethelredan and later structures have been removed to reveal the Arthurian-period defence, Rampart E, the Stony Bank (pp. 174–6). The roughly-revetted rear of this has been uncovered (compare Plate 74), while at the extreme right of the trench is a neater stretch of secondary revetment for Rampart E. The lowest part of the trench has just reached Iron Age levels. The right-hand side of the trench is the section which is drawn as *Fig. 7*.

The hill in the background gives an impression of what the Cadbury hill would have looked like before the construction of the defences.

74 The core and rear revetment of the Stony Bank, Rampart E, as revealed in Cutting D, showing evidence for the timber framework against which the stones had been piled. The two-metre ranging pole lies parallel to a longitudinal timber-slot, its tip lies against a transverse slot, and a black shadow marks a vertical one (pp. 103, 176). This is the kind of evidence on which the reconstruction of the Arthurian defences (*Fig. 29*) is based

75 The south-west gate at the start of the 1970 season, looking inwards (p. 104). In the centre background is the road surface of the late sixth century AD, with the timber slots of the Arthurian gate just visible as dark streaks across it (compare Plates 77, 78). To the left of the passage-way is the Arthurian walling seen in close-up in Plate 76. In front of this is a stretch of Ethelredan walling. For the plan of these phases see *Fig. 35*

76 The Arthurian-period walling at the south-west gate. Hammer-dressed slabs of lias lie upon large rough blocks of Jurassic limestone. Two vertical timber slots are indicated by the one-metre rods. In the background, the inverted bucket and the finds trays rest on the sixth-century road

77, 78 An early stage in the exploration of the Arthurian gateway, looking across the passage-way and outwards down the passage-way (pp. 104–5). The road surface is that of the late sixth century AD. The gaps where the sill-beams of a timber gate-tower have decayed are well-defined. Both Arthurian and Ethelredan walling is in place. For a plan see *Fig. 35*

79, 80 The first stage in the removal of the late-sixth-century road surface uncovered an iron axe-hammer and a circular buckle or brooch, seen here in the positions in which they were found (p. 104). Scale of centimetres. The buckle, one inch diameter, is of silver, with a bronze pin, now broken. It is ornamented on both faces with disintegrated animal ornament in the sixth-century Germanic or Anglo-Saxon style. Beneath the level with the buckle and axe was an earlier road surface which could also be related to the timber gate-tower (*Figs 29* and *35*)

81 The face of the Arthurian-period Rampart E (the Stony Bank) where it was best preserved in Cutting I. The metre poles mark emplacements for vertical timbers (p. 68). Although the slabby rock is very suitable for building dry stone walling, it is evident that the front revetment of Rampart E was very shoddily built

certain pits on Sites B and P which contained complete pots and undamaged grindstones.

The pits with skull burials were especially common on Site C, at the very summit of the hill. There they cluster around a small rectangular building marked by four, or more probably six, posts. The plan suggests a simple gable-ended building, sixteen by thirteen feet, raised on four corner posts, with its ridge-tree resting on the intermediate posts. This was the first rectangular building to be recognized at Iron Age Cadbury. Bearing in mind the scarcity of such structures in the British Iron Age as it appeared in 1968, and taking account of the skull-pits in the vicinity, we interpreted this at the time as a shrine. I still find this explanation plausible because of the pits. On the other hand it would be unreasonable to extend it to cover the group of six-post buildings which we disentangled from a confusion of post-holes at the eastern end of Site T. They at least should be residential, and even if some of them belong to an early phase in the site's history, some may be as late as the Middle Iron Age.

Plates 42, 54

Fig. 11

Iron Age crafts and commerce

The leading craft-product of the Iron Age, pottery, has already been described. In terms of the available information, the next most important was textiles. The chief evidence is provided by large clay loomweights, which in this period are triangular. There are also bone bobbins and shuttles for holding woollen thread. Another implement which is traditionally assigned to the weaving industry is the long-handled, short-edged comb of bone or antler. It is thought that these 'weaving-combs' were used to pack down the weft threads on a vertical loom. There is, of course, no direct evidence for this in the Iron Age, and the anthropological parallels are ambiguous. The Navaho Indians certainly do use rather similar wooden combs for closing up the weft; but the Dakotah Indians use exactly comparable bone combs for scraping the fat from animal skins. It is interesting here to recall that the densest distribution of 'weaving-combs' is in those inland regions whose inhabitants, according to Julius Caesar, were clothed in skins: *interiores . . . pellibus sunt vestiti.*[40]

Plates 56, 58

Other crafts are well-exemplified by a hoard of iron objects, of the Late phase, which was found buried in the back of Bank 1 in Cutting D. This displays the skill of the blacksmith and the range of his products in the first century BC. The masterpiece is a large felling axe, of a size such as a forester might use today. The carpenter is represented by a saw blade, and the farmer

Plates 59, 61

by a bill-hook or slasher and three sickles. In its ironwork the hoard symbolizes peaceful and productive pursuits; and it is perhaps in this light we should interpret the baked clay sling bolts which had corroded on to the saw and one of the sickles. These are usually taken to be the principal armament of the Late Iron Age; but we should occasionally remember that David was a simple herdsman before he became a warrior.[41]

Plate 59

One other object in the hoard deserves particular mention – a bar of iron, parallel-sided for most of its length, but pinched in at one end. This is an example of a class of object which is common in the first century BC in the western half of southern England: the currency bar.[42] These are iron bars of more or less standard shape, normally just over thirty inches long and weighing rather over twenty ounces. They appear to correspond with the iron rods of definite weight which, so Caesar says, were used for money by the Britons of his day.[43] It is clear from the archaeological evidence that the bars were recognized as tokens of wealth, for they were frequently deposited in hoards. And even if we do not think of them as money in our sense of the term, we may reasonably regard them as standard units in a barter system. We have already recognized hints of trade in the Glastonbury pottery at Cadbury. The currency bars – for there are fragments of others from the site as well – show the beginnings of commerce.

Fine metalworking

Plates 51, 52
Fig. 22

The iron hoard from Trench D represents the general level of competence which was at the service of the peasant farmer, but an altogether higher level is reflected by a fragmentary bronze shield fitting from Site N. This had originally been mounted on a Celtic shield, covering the boss which protected the hand grip, and extending lengthwise over a stiffening rib.[44] It is of thin sheet bronze, ornamented in relief with designs which were first hammered up from the back and then sharpened up on the front with a small chisel-like tool known as a tracer. The pattern consists of multi-dimensional curves in the high style of British Celtic art, with here and there a suggestion of animal forms – a puffin-like head with a large staring eye, for instance. Even in its sadly damaged state, this is a very notable addition to the repertory of Celtic art applied to military gear; and it gains added importance from being one of the very few pieces discovered in a hillfort. It is not the only noteworthy piece of Celtic art to be found at Cadbury. Two other objects may be singled out for mention here. From a pit on Site C came a bronze pendant, a ring with part of its circumference narrowed

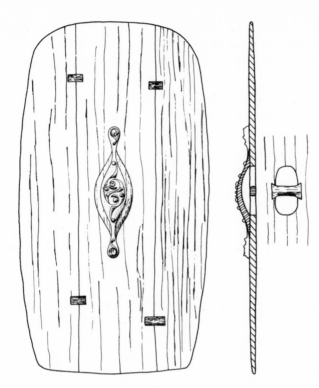

22 The decorated bronze shield-mount shown in position on the wooden boss of a characteristic Iron Age shield. The boss protects the hand-grip, as can be seen in the section and rear view of the grip (see Plates 51, 52)

down to take a loop of leather or cloth. The centre of the ring is embellished in relief with two birds' heads, with bulging eyes made of coral or paste, and up-turned bills which point towards a third boss. On the flat back of the pendant, the same basic design is outlined in engraved or chased lines. Secondly, in unstratified debris in front of the south-west gate we found a bronze disk which had evidently been cut, rather crudely, from a larger object of sheet metal. Artfully curved to conform to the circle was a very stylized animal – most probably a horse – with dumpy head, sinuous body, a pair of stick-like legs, and a long flowing tail. The legs can be compared with those of the horse-designs on the gold and silver coins of the last century of the British Iron Age, but the composition here is more sophisticated than that on the normal run of coins. We can only wonder what the original object, from which our disk was cut, had been like.

There is some evidence to show that fine objects of this kind were being produced by armourers and other craftsmen at Cadbury itself. The shield boss had been broken anciently, and had come to be buried where we found it as scrap. Another obvious piece of scrap was a shield fitting which had been twisted violently to wrench it away from the nails which had fastened it. These, and other pieces of scrap bronze and iron had been collected together

Plates VIII, IX

Plate XI

Fig. 25

Plate 55

for re-working, and then deposited beside a group of furnaces on Site N. Scattered over the same area we found a number of bronze-workers' tools: punches, tracers and scribers of both bronze and iron. Taken altogether, these imply the existence of a workshop on the Cadbury hill. This is the first time that such evidence has been found within a hillfort, and it is obviously of importance when we try to assess the fort in sociological terms.

The status and function of the Iron Age town

In outlining the basic policy of the Cadbury-Camelot excavations in Chapter Three, I have already mentioned some of the obvious questions about the character and purpose of hillforts which we hoped to answer.[45] The first concerned the permanency of occupation. In theory there are three basic possibilities: a fort may have been occupied only as a place of refuge at a time of tribal warfare; or it may have been used seasonally – perhaps in the summer season of upland grazing and cattle-raiding as I believe was the case with some upland forts in Wales; or it may have been inhabited as continuously as any Roman or medieval town. The evidence of substantial buildings at Cadbury rules out straight away the hypothesis of a temporary refuge. In itself it does not necessarily disprove the possibility of seasonal use. In the Himalaya today, for instance, the summer houses of migratory transhuming peoples are both permanent and more or less as substantial as their winter houses. But there is no reason to imagine that the Celtic farmers of southern Britain had any need to practise transhumance: a sufficient range of terrain for the practice of mixed farming was close at hand. All the weight of evidence at Cadbury – the large and permanent buildings, the storage pits, the practice of both domestic industries and more specialized crafts – point to the permanent occupation of the Late Iron Age town.

What was the status of the inhabitants in terms of rank and wealth? In the past there has been a tendency to think of hillforts as the equivalent of barons' castles. Personally, I thought that this was an unhappy concept, because it introduced anachronistic and utterly inappropriate medieval ideas into early Celtic society. Moreover, there was nothing to support it in the available archaeological evidence, apart from the defences themselves. On the contrary, the absence of prestige finds and activities – fine metalwork in particular – from hillforts argued that the social level of their inhabitants was lowly. This view is now impossible to maintain in the face of the Cadbury evidence. It is true that the discovery of the weapons and bronze finery of warrior aristocrats does not of itself prove the presence of such warriors on a site where both the bronzes and the weapons appear as scrap. All we really have evidence for is armourers and high-class craftsmen. In post-Roman Celtic society, however, we know that such craftsmen worked at the courts of princes and chieftains; and if we can project back over six or seven centuries, the Cadbury armourers and bronze-smiths similarly imply the existence of noble patrons.

Plates 50–52

Was it the warrior nobility who lived in ·the large round-houses in the centre of the fort? And are the houses which have been uncovered around the periphery of other forts significantly smaller, simply because they were the dwellings of peasants or serfs, the dependants of the nobility? It is perhaps consistent with this theory that an arc of drainage gully found immediately behind the rampart in Cutting A may have enclosed a house as small as thirteen feet in dimeter. On the other hand, in hillforts where houses are still visible today, such as Hod Hill in Dorset, and several forts in Caernarvonshire,[46] there are no marked differences in size – certainly none which might suggest differences in social status. And one of the two houses uncovered on the northern slopes (Site B) at Cadbury was nearly as large as those in the centre of the fort. On present evidence it would be very unwise to equate house size and social status, whether at Cadbury or elsewhere.

Plate 38

Fig. 10, 24

Another of our hopes had been to estimate the Iron Age population of the fort. This expectation had been fostered by the apparent ease with which the geophysical survey indicated round-houses. We confidently expected to say 'There are x circular anomalies, and therefore x round-houses: if we allow ten persons to a house, the population was 10x; if twenty persons, then 20x; and so on'. On this basis, we could at least have stated the limits of the population. But as the geophysical survey proceeded, it became obvious that the detection of irregularities decreased as we moved away from the summit, and the peripheral zone was completely blanketed by deep hill-wash. At the same time, the extensive excavation of the plateau showed that, even under optimum conditions, only about half of the buildings uncovered by excavation had been indicated by geophysical anomalies. As a result, we have no means, short of total excavation, of establishing how many houses there were at Cadbury. An analysis of the excavated storage pits, extended by a count of the unexcavated pits revealed by air-photography or geophysical survey, might in the long-term provide a basis for calculating the total food-storage capacity of the fort. On this we might build a shaky estimate of the population. But at present, there is no honest basis for calculating its size.

Fig. 6

Cf. Figs. 6, 10

Two other features of the Iron Age town deserve mention here. Firstly, it was a centre for industry and trade. The industry included both fine metal-working for the nobility, and also the cottage industries of the potter, the weaver and the blacksmith. Trade is implied by the occurrence of bronze on the site, and by sophisticated pottery in the best Glastonbury style. The currency bars indicate an organized system of barter, and anticipate the true coinage which we shall see in the next chapter. Secondly the town was a religious centre. Here again the evidence of the six-post shrine and the associated skull-burials will be reinforced in Chapter Seven. It had long been suspected that Iron Age forts had served a ritual purpose: the proof came from extensive excavations in the central area, which revealed that the focal point of the whole settlement was religious.

VII   Celtic climax and downfall

The end of the Iron Age: historical evidence

The most striking event in the Iron Age history of Cadbury is represented in the archaeological evidence by the bodies found at the south-west gate. With them was a large number of weapons, and the whole scene suggested a battle at the gate, followed by a massacre of men, women and children. From our knowledge of other hillforts in southern England, it was reasonable to suggest that the defenders were the native Celtic peoples, and their assailants the invading Romans.[47] To be more precise, it seemed that Cadbury had been stormed by the Roman army, at a date not far removed from the invasion of AD 43. Those inhabitants who had not fallen to Roman spears and swords were driven out of the fort, and the hill-top was then demilitarized by pulling down the defences and burning the gates. Evidence from Site B showed that a small task force had encamped briefly on the hill in order to carry out this destruction, and had taken the opportunity to repair equipment which had been damaged in battle. These events put an end to Celtic life and culture in about AD 45, and a firm line could be drawn across the history of the site at that point.

The key to the chronology which I have just outlined lies in the writings of the Latin biographer Suetonius, who composed a series of Lives of the Emperors early in the second century AD. One of his subjects was Vespasian, emperor from AD 69 to 79, who in the years after AD 43 had commanded the Second Augustan Legion on the left wing of the Roman advance across southern Britain. Suetonius tells us that Vespasian 'fought thirty battles, conquered two warlike tribes, and captured more than twenty towns' – the Latin word is *oppida* – 'as well as the Isle of Wight'.[48] Clear archaeological evidence from the Dorset hillforts of Maiden Castle and Hod Hill shows that these were two of the *oppida*.[49] There is also general agreement that the Durotriges, the people of Dorset and parts of Wiltshire and Somerset, were one of the two tribes. Cadbury Castle is one of some fifteen or twenty large hillforts in the territory of the Durotriges, so it has an obvious claim to be yet another of the twenty *oppida* which Vespasian captured.[50]

Fig. 2

Fig. 26

This historical hypothesis is very attractive, but from the moment we began to uncover the massacre at the gate there were difficulties in reconciling it with the whole of the archaeological evidence. Along with the bodies and the weapons were well over a hundred brooches of bronze, of many varied types. All of them had been developed, either in Britain or on the continent from Celtic types of brooch; but some varieties had only previously been found in circumstances which suggested a date after AD 43. This dating was not beyond question, for at the key sites, Camulodunum-Colchester and Hod Hill, the Roman occupation had been preceded by native Celtic activity.[51] Moreover, continental evidence suggested that these brooches should really be dated earlier than British scholars have normally allowed.[52] On balance, the evidence of the brooches was too ambiguous to prove one date rather than another for the massacre.

Plate 11

Fig. 23

What tipped the scales decisively was the evidence of the pottery. In the course of the excavations, during our examination of the finds, we had been struck by the scarcity of Roman vessels characteristic of the first and second centuries AD, and we had concluded that early Roman activity had been restricted to a very brief Conquest phase. (Incidentally, the coins supported this hypothesis. The only early coins were two very worn silver coins of the Roman Republic, and two bronze ones of the Emperor Claudius datable AD 42–54, both in mint condition, and both appropriate to the Conquest period.[53]) The most useful pottery for dating evidence is a glossy red table-ware, manufactured in Gaul and known to archaeologists as 'Samian' ware. Fairly rapid changes in shape, ornament and fabric make it possible to date Samian with some precision. When the Cadbury Samian had been studied in detail, we were surprised to learn that the reign of Nero (AD 54–68) was more strongly represented than that of his predecessor Claudius. Moreover, the Samian vessels used on Site B by the Roman troops engaged in destroying the Cadbury defences and repairing their own equipment did not date, as we expected, to the 40s; they were not earlier than the 70s.[54]

In other words, if the Roman activity on Site B was to be connected with that at the gate, then the massacre had occurred about thirty years later than we had originally assumed. This, of course, would fit the conventional dating of the brooches. Was there any other evidence to confirm it? A very close examination of the pottery found in the same level as the brooches and the bodies showed that most of it was perfectly normal native Durotrigian; but there were also fragments in a fine pale grey ware, microscopically distinguishable from Durotrigian wares, and undoubtedly early Roman in

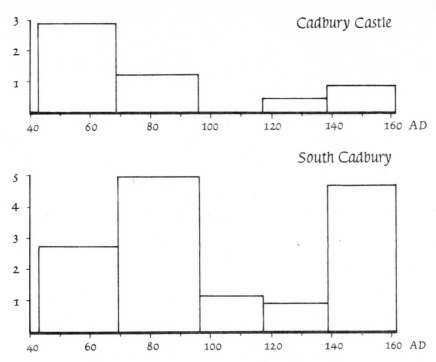

23 Relative chronology of Samian pottery from Cadbury Castle and South Cadbury village. The histograms show the average number of sherds per decade. Statistical presentation by P. J. Ashmore from information supplied by G. Dannell

date. At this stage in the development of our ideas, we came to realize that almost every large group of Durotrigian pottery which we had found contained a few uncharacteristic pieces which were either certainly or probably Roman.

The conclusions from the evidence, so far as we have studied it, are these. The Celtic culture of Cadbury was not brought to an abrupt end about AD 44. It continued to flourish for a generation or so, accepting a few material objects from the Romans, but basically unchanged from its native ways. The real break comes in the 70s. Until then, we can regard Durotrigian culture as a unity, albeit one that develops with the passage of time. This is how I propose to deal with it in the sections which follow.

The ultimate phase in the defences

It is necessary first to retrace our steps from the end of the Ultimate, or Durotrigian, phase at Cadbury to its beginning. Beneath the stonework of the final Iron Age gateway was a thin dark layer, which appeared to be humus. On the right-hand side of the gate, this layer ran up from the passage-way towards the crest of the rampart in a gentle slope. If it is correctly interpreted as humus, then it implies that immediately before the stones of the Ultimate entrance were laid, there was here a grassy bank. This in turn implies a phase of neglect, even of complete dereliction, at the gate. Can we go further and argue that the residents of an inhabited fort would never have allowed a key-point in their defences to lapse into this condition? And is the corollary that the fortified town had been abandoned for a spell before the last gate was built? We shall see shortly that the Ultimate phase saw a marked changed in pottery, in houses, and in the use of storage pits, so there is a cumulative case that late in the first century B C Cadbury had been abandoned. We do not know the reasons for the abandonment, but the fort was re-occupied early in the first century A D by people whose material culture differed strongly from that of the Late Iron Age occupants.

There is considerable evidence that the defences were reconstructed when the fort was re-occupied. The pottery found on the very bottom of Ditch 1 was of the Ultimate phase, which implies that earlier silt and rubbish had been cleaned out of the ditch. Beyond this, we can infer that the ditch was deepened as well, because the rock which was quarried from it was then used to build a massive wall at the front of the pre-existing bank. No doubt the wall originally had a sheer outer face, but this was later thrown down into the ditch, and only the rear stonework was preserved. At the same time Banks 3 and 4 were both heightened, which implies, of course, re-cutting in Ditches 2 and 3. Even from such shattered remains as the Roman working party left intact, it was clear that the last major defence-work of the Iron Age was extremely formidable.

Plates 33, 34, 36, 37

Fig. 12

The contemporary gateway was also characterized by the use of exceptionally large stones. On the right-hand side, the attempt to cope with the wearing down of the road was finally abandoned, and the guard-chamber on that side was walled off and filled in solid with rubble. On top of this was laid a platform of great slabs, which may have been a base for a look-out platform or tower. The left-hand guard-chamber was retained, in the form of a semi-circular hollow scooped out of the solid rock, faced with a skin of dry stonework, and roofed with a light covering of wicker-work. Down the passage from the guard-chamber was the single gate. This had two leaves of uneven size, turning on sturdy timber posts: the one wide enough to admit carts and chariots, the other only sufficient for pedestrians and led animals. From the gate, the stonework of the entrance passage ran forward so as to link the inner bank with Bank 2, which was extended as a hornwork to cover the direct approach to the entrance.

The Durotrigian town

It seems likely that traders' booths and stalls stood just inside the town gate, to catch the attention of rustics and their wives as they brought their goods to market. This, at least, is the most reasonable explanation for the scores of bronze brooches which were scattered down the length of the entrance – that they had come from a trinket-stall, which had been overthrown in the course of the final struggle at the gate. But we know nothing for certain about houses in the town itself. Whenever there is evidence from stratification or associated finds, the round-houses all belong to the Middle and Late phases, while the six-posters on Site T may be earlier still.

If we ask what a house of the Ultimate Iron Age might have been like in this part of Britain, the best evidence is provided by the contemporary homestead of Tollard Royal in north Dorset.[55] There the single house was clearly defined by a cluster of post-holes, irregularly spaced and of varying size and depth, forming a rough circle seventeen feet in diameter. It is not certain whether these mark the wall-line, or an inner ring of roof supports. What is certain is that at Cadbury it would have been impossible to distinguish sets of post-holes as irregular as these amid the overall complexity. It is just possible that two clusters of this kind were definable on Site C in 1968, but neither of them produced finds appropriate to the Ultimate phase. The simple truth is that we have no evidence for the character of the dwellings in the first century A D.

Fig. 10, 4, 5

Another phenomenon at this time is the scarcity of storage pits. It is true that many pits have Ultimate pottery in their topmost layer, but this merely indicates that they still existed as shallow depressions in which rubbish might accumulate. Only a very small number produce Ultimate pottery throughout their filling. I have already commented on the scarcity of pits in the Early phase, and I suggested that we had not located the main focus of the Early settlement. But this hypothesis is unnecessary in the Ultimate phase. The storage pits at Maiden Castle had all been filled in by this time, so we are faced with a general phenomenon. A probable explanation is that very large pottery store jars had become available, and these must have been far more convenient than the pits.

Despite the absence of identifiable houses, one building can certainly be attributed to the Ultimate phase, namely the porched shrine which stands at the mid-point of the axial ridge. The quantity of Ultimate pottery which had been tamped down into the wall trench leaves no room for doubt about the cultural phase to which it belongs, but two particular fragments of pot and an iron arrow-head suggest that the date is after rather than before

Plates 48, 49
Fig. 10, 27

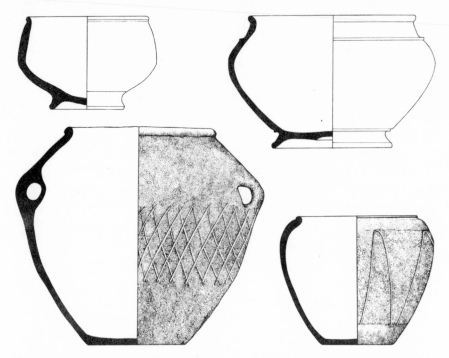

24 Restored vessels of the Ultimate Iron Age phase. A bead-rim bowl of the type found in the Maiden Castle war cemetery; a jar with countersunk handles; a sophisticated cordonned bowl; and a simple bead-rim bowl. The jar is 9 ins high

AD 43. The inner room of the shrine was about eight feet square. On the east was a doorway just over three feet wide, opening on to a porch or verandah nearly four feet deep. It is possible that the porched shrine replaced a simpler and less substantial building a few feet further east. If this is correct, the earlier shrine may go back before AD 43. Immediately outside it a full-grown cow had been buried. Beyond this again, conforming to the axis of the porched shrine, and bounded on the south by a wooden fence, was the zone with burials of young animals. To the north of the axial line were the supposed weapon-burials, mostly disturbed by ploughing. If these are correctly interpreted, we may see here the offerings of peasant and of warrior either side of a processional approach to the shrine.

Plate 45

Crafts and Commerce

Fig. 24

The pottery of the Ultimate Iron Age phase at Cadbury is distinguished by technical competence and aesthetic dullness. It includes bowls with bead-rims, developed from the varied bead-rim bowls of the Late Iron Age by a process of simplification and standardization. Then there are larger bowls, with a highly polished black surface, ornamented with horizontal ridges or cordons. Both the bead-rim and the cordoned bowls often stand on foot-rings. Medium-sized jars may have either bead-rims or upright necks, and they frequently have thick loop handles which are partly countersunk into the body of the jar. The jars commonly have simple lattice ornament on the body. Most of this pottery is hard-fired and thin-walled. The fossil shell filler of earlier pottery has now given way to sand-gritted fabric. Finally, most pieces were finished, if not actually thrown, on a fast potter's wheel.

Taken as a whole, this Ultimate pottery compares well with that deposited, about AD 44, in the well-known War Cemetery at Maiden Castle.[56] It is usually regarded as characteristic of the tribe of the Durotriges, but I have reservations about the equation of tribe and ceramic group in this particular instance. It is generally considered that the technically less sophisticated pottery of earlier generations had been made in the home by the women-folk, and in that case it probably did represent tribal taste and culture quite faithfully. But when the fast wheel was introduced, potting ceased to be a domestic craft and became a specialized industry, removed from the home and divorced from the tribe. It is worth noticing here that the skill of Durotrigian potters was so highly regarded by the conquering Romans that they exploited it to meet both military and civilian needs. The pottery found on Hadrian's Wall from AD 122 is directly descended from that current in Dorset a century earlier. For these reasons, we cannot say whether the Ultimate pottery at Cadbury implies that the site fell within the political boundaries of the Durotriges, or whether the town was at the receiving end of a vigorous trade from more southerly areas.

We have already seen that after the Roman conquest and occupation of southern England, new types of pottery became available at Cadbury. The most obvious was the Samian table-ware, for its glossy red surface must have been conspicuous against the predominant blacks and greys of Durotrigian pottery. But the total quantity available to the inhabitants of Cadbury was minute: in our five seasons of excavation we found fragments of less than a dozen Samian vessels of this period. Another interesting introduction was that of cream or pink coloured jugs in an exceptionally hard fabric, for these had been manufactured in kilns set up at Corfe Mullen (near Wimborne Minster, Dorset) immediately after the Conquest:[57] the Romans were obviously exploiting and developing the existing talents of the Durotrigian potters. Yet another innovation was that of very large, heavy storage jars. These novelties formed only a very small component in the Ultimate Iron Age pottery at Cadbury: by and large, the vessels available to an ordinary household changed little in the generation after AD 43.

25 Coin series showing the development and derivation of Celtic coinage from the gold stater of Philip II of Macedon (359–336 BC). His stater has the head of Apollo (obverse) and a racing chariot with the legend ΦΙΛΙΠΠΟΥ (reverse). The design is copied and breaks up, but is still recognisable, on a gold stater of the Parisii of Gaul; it then becomes a very degenerate copy on a stater of the British Durotriges. The last coin is an example of a Durotrigian stater of this type found at Cadbury (see Plate 57)

Plates 11, 57
Fig. 1

The occurrence of industrially-produced pottery throughout the Ultimate phase is, of course, evidence for trade. Beyond this, an increase in commercial activity is demonstrated by the Celtic coins from Cadbury. For the most part, the coins are of types found widely in the territory of the Durotriges, so once again they raise the question whether their presence at Cadbury denotes the extent of Durotrigian political influence, or whether they are merely evidence for some kind of commercial activity. Even in commercial terms, their significance is ambiguous, because there are no bronze coins to provide small denominations. This statement is at variance with the traditional account of Durotrigian coinage, which is that in the pre-Roman period the tribe had struck both silver and bronze coins. At first sight we had examples of both metals at Cadbury: but chemical treatment showed that all but one of the apparent bronze coins were in fact of silver, of varying degrees of purity. The exception was certainly bronze, but it appeared to be a core for a gold-plated forgery. It is consequently difficult to believe that the coins represent a true money economy.[58]

Fig. 25

The Durotrigian coins are barbarous affairs, which have travelled a long road of degeneration from the prototype gold stater of Philip II of Macedon. Among the Durotriges, the head of Apollo, which should form the obverse, has become a meaningless scatter of dots. On the reverse, the chariot and horses have also disintegrated into lines, representing the horses' legs, and blobs for everything else. In complete contrast is a gold stater, inscribed ANTEθ RIG, 'King Antethos'. Antethos was a ruler of the Dobunni, a tribe which inhabited the Cotswolds and the Lower Severn valley in the decades before the Roman Conquest.[59] Cadbury lies close to the southern boundary of the distribution of Dobunnic coins, and in a similar relationship to the northern boundary of those of the Durotriges, so it is not surprising that coins of both tribes have been found on the site. The Antethos coin bears a stylized ear of grain, looking rather like a Christmas tree, on the obverse. On the reverse is a horse, stylized in the Celtic manner, but none-theless both recognizable and lively. Beneath its belly is one wheel of the original chariot.

Native Durotrigian coins probably continued to circulate after AD 43, especially in the form of cast bronze issues, which provided small change for minor commercial transactions. None of these cast coins have been found at Cadbury, however, and their absence, together with the scarcity of early Roman coins, shows that money played very little part in the economy of the site in the mid-first century. It is even possible that the two Claudian bronze coins which we found had been lost by troops of the military working party in the 70s, though their near-mint condition tells against this suggestion.

Metalwork and art

For the most part, the Durotrigian metalwork found at Cadbury came from the massacre and destruction levels at the south-west gate. Consequently it represents the kind of metalwork that was current among native communities during the first generation of the Roman occupation of southern England. Any piece is therefore likely to reflect, in greater or lesser degree, the taste of the conquerors, rather than a purely Celtic style. The artistic ambiguity which results is well demonstrated by the bronze plaque which was found on the floor of the guard-chamber of the Ultimate gate, beneath a layer of burned and collapsed roofing.

The plaque was a sheet of very thin bronze, beaten out from behind to produce a human face in relief. I say human, but it is at least as likely that it is intended to represent a divine or demonic personage. About this description there can be no disagreement, nor can it be disputed that the plaque was in the possession of the Celtic inhabitants of Cadbury at the time of the Roman assault: its stratified position guarantees that. But when we try to

Plate XII

assess its cultural and aesthetic background, argument is rife. One school of opinion, impressed by the general scarcity of human representations in Celtic art, and by the lively realism of some aspects of our piece, regards it as classical in inspiration and Roman in workmanship. Some would even identify it with Medusa. Another school points to the stylistic features which can be paralleled in such Celtic figural art as we possess: the frontality, the character of the eyes, the stylization of the curls. The explanation probably lies in taking an element of truth from each, and seeing the plaque as the work of a Celtic craftsman, who was heavily influenced by Roman models. It might have been made in Gaul, or even in Britain, where examples of Roman representational art were already beginning to appear in the decades before the invasion of AD 43. But whatever its artistic source, it is agreed that the plaque had ornamented a wooden chest or casket. And if we interpret it, despite its genial appearance, as a demon-mask, then it gave magical protection to whatever precious goods the chest contained.[60]

Plates 11, 65, 66

The bronze brooches which were found in such abundance at the south-west gate, and in smaller numbers in the Ultimate phase of Bank 1, also reflect the development of Celtic taste under Roman influences. Some of them were simple penannular or hoop brooches, and there can be no doubt about the Celtic origins of these. But the larger number were bow or

Fig. 26a

Fig. 26b

safety-pin brooches. Many of these have their pins sprung with wire coils in the ancient Celtic manner, whilst others, more advanced, have hinged pins. The bow is normally decorated with cast grooves and ridges, and is then further embellished by punching or engraving in the grooves to produce wave or zig-zag patterns. Some patterns are so fine that today they can only be analysed under a lens, but this does not imply that the ancient jeweller used a lens – only that he was interested in producing surface effects by minute and delicate movements of his tools.

The bow brooches all derive from types which were current in Celtic Europe, and probably in Britain too, before the beginning of the Christian era. We have already noticed, however, that some of the more developed forms have normally been found on sites like Colchester or Hod Hill where the Roman presence is stronger than the Celtic. Fortunately the evidence for their relative date and associations is fairly clear at Cadbury. When the Ultimate rampart was built some decades before AD 43, several brooches were dropped and became incorporated in the bank along with purely

Fig. 26c, d

Durotrigian pottery. These brooches all have straight-sided, slightly tapered bows. Immediately before the Roman assault in the 70s, the rampart was hastily refurbished. More brooches were incorporated in it, and with them

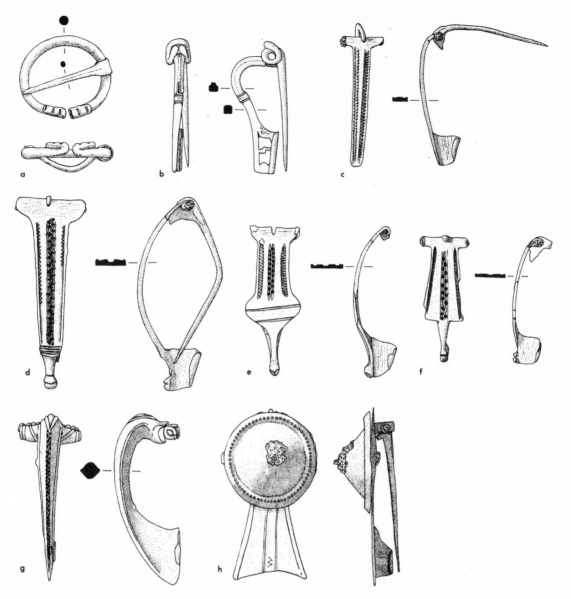

26 *Bronze brooches of the Ultimate Iron Age.* a *simple penannular;* b *safety-pin or bow-brooch with sprung pin;* c, d *hinged brooches typical of the last decades of the pre-Roman Iron Age, but continuing in use for some decades after the Roman invasion of AD 43;* e, f, g *types introduced around the middle of the first century AD, and characteristic of the massacre level at the south-west gate;* h *an unusually elaborate brooch, with a hollow conical head of tinned bronze.* c–h *are all decorated with various forms of chased and punched ornament.* d *is 2⅝ ins long*

was both Durotrigian pottery and also Roman pottery including Samian. The brooches from this level included some with wings on the bow – a characteristic of the brooches from Hod Hill. The brooches from the massacre at the gate include both straight-tapered and winged bows,

Fig. 26e

showing that the pre-Roman type had not been driven off the market by later Romanized fashions.

Plate 63

Another major class of metalwork is represented by the iron weapons which were found along with the brooches and corpses. Indeed, it is the weapons which provide the principal evidence for a battle at the gate. The commonest are large leaf-shaped spear blades, which probably served as the heads of pikes. They form a well-known type among the pre-Roman Britons. More unusual are two spears with small flat heads and long thin shanks. These could possibly be feeble imitations of the *pilum* used by Roman legionaries – a javelin with a shaft which was designed to bend or break on striking an enemy shield. There are also two bowl-shaped shield bosses. Although we might expect both the attackers and the defenders to have lost weapons, none which we found could be assigned to Roman legionaries. On the other hand, any of them might have been used by Roman auxiliary troops, for these could have included Celtic horsemen recruited in Gaul, and using weapons very similar to those of their cousins in Britain. Another attribute of the Celtic warrior is the metal neck-ring or torc. These are frequently of bronze or even gold, but in the gateway we found two ex-

Plates 64, X

amples of iron. One of these is remarkable as being the earliest instance in Britain of the use of brass for an ornamental inlay.

The Roman assault

The fate of the native Britons at the hands of Vespasian's legion varied from one *oppidum* to another. At Maiden Castle there was a battle involving both an artillery bombardment and hand-to-hand fighting. On their defeat, the inhabitants were left to bury their dead amid the outworks of the east entrance. After some lapse of time, the gates and the walling of the passage-way were dismantled, and the inhabitants were removed to the new low-land town of Durnovaria – Dorchester. At Hod Hill there is evidence for an artillery bombardment, but none for close combat or massacre. Neverthe-less, the inhabitants were immediately turned out of the fort, and a Roman garrison was planted in their place in a regularly laid out auxiliary fort.

Cadbury, by contrast, was evidently by-passed in the mid-40s. The inhabitants continued to live in their ancestral manner, taking very little from the Romans: a little Gaulish table-ware, some fine jugs from the Corfe Mullen kiln, perhaps a few coins, and the latest fashions in brooches. Some of them seem to have moved down the hill to found the first settlement in South Cadbury itself, for an independent excavation directed by Mr John

Fig. 3

Laidlaw showed that rectangular timber buildings were being erected there in the 50s. Life certainly continued within the defences; intensive traffic through the south-west gate is demonstrated by the wearing down of the road surface. And it was probably during the generation after the invasion that the porched shrine replaced a simpler shrine on the summit ridge.

Why was the peaceful continuity of native life so violently shattered in the 70s? The question is not at all easy to answer within the framework of our current knowledge of early Romano-British history. If we could date the Roman assault to the early 60s, we could see it as a local reflection of the great revolt of Queen Boudicca, and the severe repression which followed it. But the Roman activity on Site B is dated to the 70s (or even later) by the Samian pottery found there, so the Boudiccan rising is ruled out. In the late 60s and 70s the focus of military activity in Britain shifted northwards, and at the same time the natives were encouraged to settle in newly founded towns as part of a policy of civilizing them. For instance, the Roman garrison evacuated the fort at Dorchester, and the inhabitants of Maiden Castle were then moved down to establish a town there. Is it possible that the people of Cadbury Castle resisted an attempt to civilize them, and had to be forcibly transplanted? There is this at least in favour of thé hypothesis, that the evidence suggests police action – albeit of a brutal kind – rather than a full-scale military campaign.

Whatever the reason for the Roman assault, it is clear that the natives were forewarned and had made preparations to resist it. I have already mentioned that Bank 1 had been refurbished. This was done by scraping up soil from inside the defences, and piling it on top of the existing rampart. At the south-west entrance, three large pits were dug outside the gate itself. Clear traces of burning showed that posts had been standing in the pits at the time of the attack, and it is likely that they supported an arrangement of barricades across the passage-way. Needless to say, these crude emergency measures were unavailing against superior Roman discipline and weaponry. Some of the inhabitants were slain at the gate, and their bodies were left to rot where they had fallen. Others were removed to the lowlands, either to the settlements at Catsgore and Ilchester, seven miles away, or simply to South Cadbury, where there is a marked intensification of activity from this time on.

Fig. 7
Fig. 12

Fig. 23

Plate 36

Subsequently the Roman police party returned to Cadbury to complete its work by burning the timberwork of the gate and pulling down the stone-work of the entrance-passage and the defences. The thoroughness of their demolition is revealed by the disappearance of the Ultimate revetment of

Plates 70–72

Bank 1 and the corresponding occurrence of masses of stone thrown down into Ditch 1. In the interior, traces of the working party were recovered in profusion around an area of burned clay, probably the base of a field oven, on Site B. Numerous fragmentary bronzes from armour suggest that the troops were having to repair equipment which had been damaged in their police action. There were ornamental disks, probably from helmets; bindings from shields; buckles from leather equipment; hinge-plates from leather or metal cuirasses; and most spectacular of all, bronze links from a harness-suite, inlaid in silver.

Plate X

Plate 69

Fig. 10, 30

It is possible that the working-party was living in tents, but more likely that it had been housed in the small rectangular buildings that we discovered on the western side of Site B. Within the limits of our excavation, we traced three of these, set in a row beside the hollow-way, but it is quite likely that there were others downhill from the ones which we found. They were each about twenty feet long by thirteen feet wide, and they were separated one from another by a thirteen-foot gap. It was this regularity of lay-out which suggested that these were Roman military buildings, despite the lack of exact parallels on known Roman forts. Although the huts were erected on a slope, nothing had been done to dig out level emplacements for them. On the other hand, structural details suggested that they had raised – and therefore level – wooden floors. Finally, whether we accept these as the barracks of the Roman working party, or think of it as occupying a tented camp, there is no evidence at all that it was protected by defences of a Roman military pattern. This seems consistent with the hypothesis that we are dealing with police action rather than with a military campaign.

Cadbury during the Roman period

Fig. 23

After the forcible removal of its inhabitants, the Cadbury hill-top was probably given over to agriculture. The only datable material which spans the next two centuries consists of five scraps of Samian, which had probably come in with manure from the middens of the settlement at the foot of the hill. That settlement continued to flourish through the remainder of the first and much of the second century. Mr Laidlaw's research showed that there were at least two structural periods in the buildings there. Unfortunately, however, the area available for excavation between modern cottages was so limited that it was not possible to work out the plans of these buildings.

By the end of the second century, to judge from the pottery and coins, activity at South Cadbury was tapering off. Some time in the later third century, however, coins and pottery begin to occur once more on the hill-top. To the handful of late Roman coins which we found must be added the hundreds which have been ploughed up and dispersed over the centuries. The most likely cause of this renewed activity is the construction of a pagan temple, if, that is, we can judge from the evidence of other hill-forts which have yielded Late Roman material. The most spectacular temple discovered by excavation is the one at Lydney in Gloucestershire, where a building of classical plan was dedicated to the Celtic god Nodens. But more typical are the simpler buildings at Maiden Castle in Dorset and Brean Down in Somerset. These are Romano-Celtic temples in the strict sense of the term: a small square shrine surrounded on all sides by a verandah. Here the ancestral Celtic gods were worshipped, their names coupled with those of the Olympic pantheon; and here devout pilgrims made offerings of votive figures, bronze trinkets, and coins.[61]

At Cadbury there is, in fact, no direct evidence for such a temple. But the inference that one had existed is very reasonably based on the Late Roman coins, which could well have been offerings. The gilt-bronze letter 'A' can be paralleled at various temple sites, so it too is a pointer. Moreover, the post-Roman defence, Rampart E, contains roofing tiles of pot and stone, and both hammer-dressed and sawn stones, all of which had been removed from some sophisticated Roman building. Bearing in mind the evidence for Iron Age shrines, we may believe that Cadbury had retained its sanctity over the centuries.

Plate 10

Plate 76

Even so, it must appear remarkable that no trace of a temple-building, or even of its robbed-out foundations, was found whether by excavation or air-photography or geophysical prospecting. A possible explanation is provided by a consideration of the Brean Down temple. There the foundations were laid directly on the solid rock, not in a rock-cut foundation trench. The hard Oolitic limestone of the Cadbury plateau would have made an ideal bedding for such foundations. And once the superstructure had been robbed to provide material for the next defence work, the subsequent centuries of ploughing and quarrying would have obliterated all remaining traces. In the sixteenth century Leland could write that 'yn dyverse places men may se fundations and rudera of walles'; but by the early eighteenth, to judge from Stukeley's account, these had vanished.[62] We can almost see the presumed Romano-Celtic temple disappearing over the intervening years.

VIII Camelot and Cadanbyrig

Dating evidence in the late fifth and sixth centuries

The latest coin that has any bearing on the Late Roman use of Cadbury is one of Honorius, datable AD 393–402. In fact the coin series at other Romano-Celtic temples usually ends before this, and it seems therefore that the pagan temples had been deserted by the end of the fourth century in face of official support for Christianity. The Honorian coin is also the latest datable object stratified beneath the first post-Roman phase of rampart building, the so-called Stony Bank or Rampart E. On its evidence, therefore, Rampart E could date as early as AD 400. If this were so, it would belong not in the Arthurian period but in a shadowy phase of very late Roman re-fortification which has been recognized at the hillfort of the Breiddin in Montgomery-shire, and perhaps also at Cadbury-Congresbury in north Somerset.[63] At

Plates 79, 80, XI

the other extreme of the dating range, we have the silver ring or buckle which lay beneath the later road of the south-west gateway through the Stony Bank defences. No close parallel is known for the form of this buckle, but there can be little doubt that its disintegrated animal ornament belongs in the last third of the sixth century. Therefore, the roadway through the gate was resurfaced about the 570s. But there is no evidence that the timber gate-tower itself needed any repairs at that time, and it is certain that its main uprights were not renewed. We do not know how long earthfast timbers of this kind might last, but it is difficult to believe that it could be more than a century. If this is correct, and if the evidence of the silver buckle has been properly assessed, then a date nearer AD 500 than 400 seems reasonable for the original Rampart E defensive scheme.

This date makes it necessary to bring the imported Tintagel-type pottery

Plate XIII

into the discussion. Three classes of this pottery were found at Cadbury

Fig. 27

Castle.[64] Class A consists of rather fine red bowls, with wall-sided rims which are often decorated with rouletting. The bases have a shallow foot-ring, and sometimes bear stamped crosses on the interior. A source in the east Mediterranean is certain, but cannot be precisely located within an arc

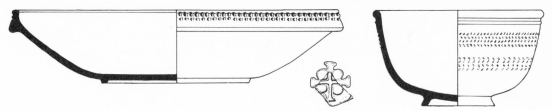

27 Restored pottery vessels of the late fifth and early sixth centuries AD; a red dish with rouletted rim imported from the eastern Mediterranean (class A); a cross-stamp from the base of a class A dish; and a grey bowl with bands of rouletted ornament, brought to Cadbury from the Bordeaux region (class D). The class A dish is 11 ins in diameter

from Greece to Egypt. Stratified deposits in Greece provide dates which can be applied to the British examples; and Dr John Hayes, who has studied the Mediterranean evidence, would place the Cadbury pieces in the period from AD 460/70 to 510/20. Class B consists of a variety of large jars, used to import wine, oil, or even dry goods. One sub-class was perhaps made on the Black Sea coast of Romania, but in general only a vague source in the eastern Mediterranean can be indicated. Some of the Cadbury examples belong to a sub-class which is datable to the fifth rather than the sixth century, but it is unlikely that these were imported before the 460s or 470s, because the western Mediterranean had been closed to traffic around the middle of the century by Vandal piracy. Finally, Class D includes various bowls in a distinctive grey fabric with a blue-black wash. It was imported from the Bordeaux region, but site evidence in Gaul tells us only that it belongs in the fifth or sixth centuries.

Fig. 28

Fig. 27

In general terms, the occurrence of this imported pottery implies that the Cadbury hill-top was re-occupied from about AD 470 by a community wealthy enough to take part in the trade which it demonstrates. Of more particular significance, a fragment from a Class B wine-jar was found in or under Rampart E, finally clinching a date in the late fifth or early sixth century for its construction. The only other firmly-stratified Tintagel-type pottery was in the wall-trench of the timber hall which will be described shortly. Slight though the evidence is, it is just enough to establish that around AD 500, Cadbury was once again a fortified place, with a large timber hall as its central building.

The defences and gate

What was the character of the new defences? For a start, of course, Cadbury enjoyed some protection from the natural steepness of the hill, and even more from the four or five lines of Iron Age banks and ditches. It is true that the ditches were partly silted up, and the banks eroded – but even today

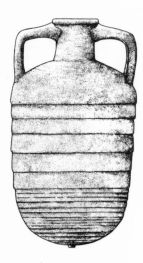

28 Examples from Egypt of amphorae which would be classed as Biv and Bii in the British Isles. No restorable amphorae have yet been found in Britain or Ireland. Scale 1 : 8

they would present formidable obstacles to an attacking force. Despite this, they were supplemented by a wholly new work, raised on the decayed top of the innermost Iron Age rampart.

The essential feature of the fifth- and sixth-century defence was a timber framework constructed of beams about six inches square. We can only infer these beams from the holes and slots which they left in the body of the rampart as they decayed, and the evidence is necessarily patchy. It shows, however, that there were vertical timbers at the front of the rampart, which were probably carried up to a breastwork of planks or wickerwork. Other vertical timbers were set in the body of the bank, and were tied to the front timbers by transverse horizontal beams. Lines of stones running parallel with the rampart face imply the existence of longitudinal ties as well. Relatively few of the vertical timbers were earthfast, so the framework took its rigidity from pegged joints, and its stability from the earth and rubble which had been piled within it. The whole scheme was finished off with a poorly constructed facing of dry stonework. Roman dressed stone and building debris was used lavishly in both the facing-wall and the rampart core.

The plan of the contemporary south-west gate was also recovered. Its main structural feature was a square (or more properly a parallelogram) of four posts. The pits for these were dug down through the debris of the Iron Age gate to a depth of over three feet, and the posts themselves were six to eight inches thick. Across the front and rear of the gate was a timber threshold also about eight inches wide, while the rampart ends were shored up at either side of the gate with sturdy planks. There is no evidence for the actual door arrangements, but it is reasonable to infer an outer and an inner gate, each of two five-foot leaves. Above the head of the door we necessarily enter into a world of speculation. The stoutness of the corner posts, and the depth to which they were bedded, imply that they were intended to support a weighty superstructure. This could have been a bridge carrying the rampart walk across the gate passage, but bearing in mind the timber gate-towers of Roman forts, it is perfectly reasonable to imagine the Cadbury gate carried up as an elevated fighting-platform, reached by a ladder from the sentry walk.[65]

Mention of possible Roman analogies prompts an analysis of the ancestry of this defensive scheme. Although Roman masonry was re-used in the rampart, the manner of its use was completely un-Roman: as dry, not mortared stonework. In fact, the combination of wood and dry stonework seems to look back to a Celtic ancestry, and in appearance there can have been little difference between Rampart B – the second phase of the Iron Age

Fig. 19
176

defences – and Rampart E in the late fifth century A D. But it is impossible to see how a knowledge of Celtic techniques of fortification could have been transmitted over the intervening centuries; and it is more likely that the post-Roman scheme at Cadbury was thought out from scratch by builders who were ignorant alike of Celtic fortification and of Roman mortared masonry. At broadly this time on the continent, people were returning to hill-tops which had originally been occupied in the Iron Age, and were defending themselves against barbarian attacks by means of ramparts of timber and stone.[66] In each case we see like causes producing like effects.

The gateway, on the other hand, definitely suggests Roman analogues. It is true that the timber gates of Roman legionary fortresses and auxiliary forts were frequently far more elaborate, with a double passage-way flanked by guard-chambers carried up as towers. But there was also a simpler form, with a single passage-way, no flanking chambers and a tower rising directly over the passage. These simple gates were often six-post structures – that is to say, with three posts either side of an elongated passage – and this type lasted throughout the first millennium to appear finally in the gate-towers of Norman earth-and-timber castles.[67] In some cases a shorter passage had only four main posts, with an extra pair inserted for the gate-hanging.[68] This four-post type is the inspiration of the Cadbury gate. It is true that the known examples come from the first century A D; but a six-post gate-tower was built at Richborough in the late third century, and timber gates of unknown form were being maintained at Forden Gaer into the fourth century. So a direct Roman ancestry is not impossible for the Cadbury gate.

The hall

Within the defences, only one building can be definitely assigned to the late fifth or sixth century: the timber hall located on Site L in 1968 and explored in 1969. I have already explained how this was dated by the freshly-broken sherds of a Class B wine-jar which had been tamped down into the filling of a wall trench. The trench itself had held a light screen or partition, which was placed one third of the way along a building with parallel sides and slightly bowed ends. The main frame of the building consisted of upright posts set at about ten foot centres. The post-holes did not penetrate very far below the present surface of the rock, which implies either that the level of the bedrock has been lowered by weathering, and especially by ploughing; or more probably that the whole structure depended on a braced timber framework rather than on earthfast posts. This would suggest similar

Plates 82–4, XIII

177

29 *Reconstruction of the Arthurian-period rampart and south-west gate-tower. For some of the evidence on which this is based, see Fig. 35*

carpentry techniques to those employed in the contemporary rampart, and it is interesting that in neither case were iron nails used. The shallowness of the main timbers also explains why only slight traces were found of a northern row of roof supports, and even less of a southern row.

Fig. 30

A plausible reconstruction of the building would suggest an infilling of wattle and daub for the walls, and a thatched roof. There was probably a door in each of the long walls, beside the screen. An open central hearth is likely in the larger room, but the evidence has been ploughed away. Two points may be emphasized about the building. Firstly, it stands in a dominant position on the axial ridge at the centre of the summit plateau as defined by the five hundred feet contour. This in itself would lead us to believe that it was the principal building of the Arthurian-period fort. Secondly, the size, sixty-three feet long by thirty-four feet wide, puts it within the size-range of medieval halls. It is smaller than the contemporary hall at Castle Dore in

Fig. 31

Cornwall, or the seventh-century royal halls at Yeavering in Northumbria. But the tenth-century royal hall at Cheddar, Somerset, was only sixty by thirty feet. Even if we interpret the smaller room, behind the partition, as a

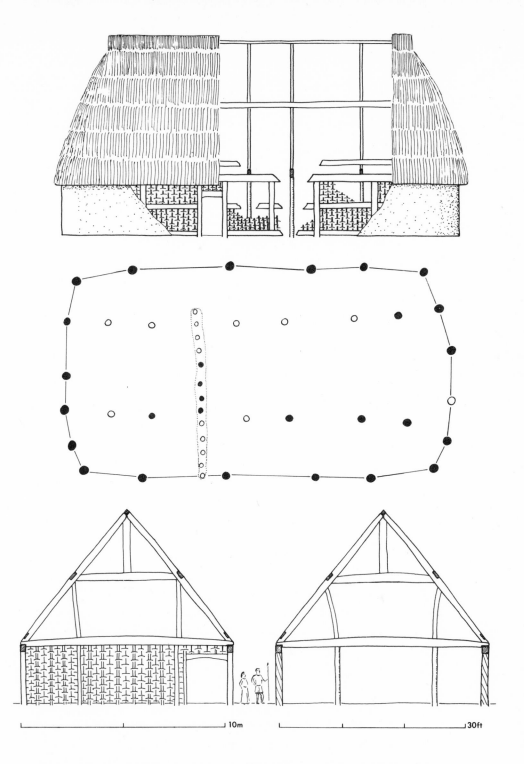

30 Reconstruction of the Arthurian-period feasting hall. Cutaway elevation, plan and two sections. On the plan, definite post-holes are shown in solid black; open circles indicate inferred posts. In the elevation and sections all minor structural elements and details of jointing have been omitted

179

private chamber, and think that the hall proper consisted only of the larger room, it is still close in size to some Oxbridge college halls.[69] On the evidence of early Welsh and English poetry, we can reasonably see this as the feasting hall of a king or war-leader of the Arthurian period.

The status of Cadbury–Camelot

Plate 85

Fig. 10, 16

This account of the defences, gate-tower and hall exhausts our information about Cadbury in the decades around AD 500. But from other sources we can postulate further evidence which we might have expected, and ask why it was not found. For a start, Welsh legal documents list the buildings which ought to form part of prince's court. In addition to the hall and private chamber, they are: a kitchen, a chapel, a barn, a kiln-house for drying grain, a stable, a porch and a privy.[70] A few yards north-east of the hall we did indeed find the wall-trenches of a building about fifteen feet long by five feet wide, which could have been a kitchen, but there is nothing to show that it belongs to this period.

Secondly, other excavated sites have been much richer in artefacts of the late fifth and sixth centuries, and in evidence for both domestic and industrial activity. The richest of the published excavations was at the small princely stronghold of Dinas Powys in Glamorgan.[71] This yielded both a greater quantity and a wider range of imported pottery than Cadbury. Among the iron objects from Cadbury, only two knives could certainly be attributed to this period, whereas at Dinas Powys we found nineteen knives or fragments of blades, as well as awls, a drill-bit, a file, fish-hooks, a bucket handle, and miscellaneous clamps, cleats and nails. At Dinas Powys, moreover, numerous crucibles provided evidence for jewel-making, an activity appropriate to a prince's court, while quantities of scrap bronze and glass provided raw material for the jeweller. Humbler crafts included leather-, textile, and bone-working. None of these activities was represented at Cadbury, or if it was, the evidence for the fifth and sixth centuries could not be isolated from that of both earlier and later periods.

At first sight, this would seem to tell against Cadbury being either important or heavily occupied. But we have to bear in mind the hazards and chances of discovery in a form of exploration where the researcher is working blind. At Dinas Powys, the total area of the site was small, and about a quarter of the interior was totally excavated. Moreover, the sixth-century rubbish dumps were located, and proved to be a bountiful source of finds. At Cadbury, by contrast, the middens of this period were not found; and

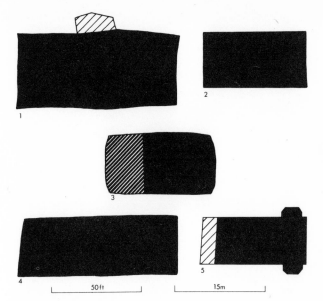

31 *Comparative floor areas of medieval halls. 1 Castle Dore, Cornwall, palace of the kings of Dumnonia (the porch is shaded); 2 Cheddar, Somerset, tenth century royal hall; 3 Cadbury-Camelot (chamber shaded); 4 Tilleda, north Germany, eleventh century feasting hall of the German emperors (after P. Grimm, in* Medieval Archaeology *12 (1968), pp. 83–100); 5 Brasenose College, Oxford, sixteenth century hall (floor area only, screens passage shaded; after RCHM Inventory of . . .* City of Oxford, *p. 24)*

although a good proportion of the summit plateau was cleared, most of the interior was not even sampled. Apart from the vicinity of the hall, the area richest in imported pottery was the south-west gate, but it was clear from the stratification that the sherds found there had washed downhill between the Arthurian and Ethelredan periods. Somewhere inside the south-west gate there must be a major focus of sixth-century activity; but since it lies buried under some eight feet of hill-wash, we did not feel justified in searching for it.

Hazards of excavation apart, it would be unreasonable to use the quantity of imported pottery as an index of the importance of a site. Castle Dore in Cornwall was a small Iron Age fortress, re-used in the post-Roman centuries, when it enclosed a timber hall about ninety feet long by forty wide. Excavations covering a large part of the interior produced only one untypical imported sherd, and no other contemporary artefacts. It has been suggested that not only had the floor levels been obliterated by ploughing, but the associated artefacts had been destroyed in the same way. This is impossible to credit in face of the material which has survived centuries of ploughing at Cadbury. Five seasons of excavation at Castell Degannwy, a royal fortress of the princes of north-west Wales, produced two definite sherds of Class B, and about ten less certain examples. At Castle Dore it is the architectural evidence, and at Castell Degannwy the historical associations, which determine the status of the site.[72] In the same way, the importance of Cadbury around AD 500 is declared not by the quantity of imported pottery recovered by excavation, but by the timber hall, the gate-tower, and the whole defensive scheme.

Figs. 31, 33

Fig. 33

The strategic role of the fortress

At this point we may speculate on the strategic role played by the new defensive work. Here we can usefully start with the second phase, represented by the re-metalling of the roadway at the south-west gate. I have argued that the silver buckle found beneath the road dates it probably to the 570s, and certainly to the last third of the sixth century. This brings us to a historically-recorded period of Anglo-Saxon expansion against the West Welsh, the inhabitants of Dumnonia, that is, modern Cornwall, Devon and Somerset. In AD 577, according to the *Anglo-Saxon Chronicle*, the rulers of Wessex, Cuthwine and Ceawlin, 'fought the Britons at the place that is called Deorham' and captured Gloucester, Cirencester and Bath. Deorham is identified with the modern Dyrham, a little north of Bath, which itself is about twenty-five miles from Cadbury. Assuming that the *Chronicle* is recording only the decisive event in a protracted campaign of Wessex aggression and British resistance, Cadbury would seem a good base for the defence of Dumnonia. Either before or after Deorham, therefore, its defences might have been put in a state of repair. There are obvious hazards in fitting the one historical record to the one archaeological fact in a period when both are scarce; but provided the hazards are recognized, the speculation is justified.

Fig. 32

If Cadbury might have served as a Dumnonian base against Wessex in the 570s, what was its role a century earlier, at the time of the first imported pottery? Before we attempt to answer this, we must compare it with other British fortresses of the late fourth and fifth centuries. It has long been recognized that in Wales and the Marches numerous Iron Age hillforts, both large and medium in size, were re-occupied during the Late Roman period. None of them, however, appeared to have been refortified, and third- and fourth-century refuse lapped over the back of the decayed ramparts. In 1969 Chris Musson started to re-explore one of them, the Breiddin. By extending the Cadbury technique of very wide rampart cuttings, he was able to show, contrary to the received view, that the Breiddin had been refortified in the late fourth century with a sophisticated timber defence, in the form of a raised fighting platform and look-out towers. It seems possible, therefore, that fuller exploration might show that such major works of refortification were common at the very end of the Roman period.

When we turn to the forts which produce the Tintagel-type of imported pottery, the picture is very different. At present we know about a dozen such sites used by the Britons. Many of them are re-used Iron Age hillforts,

Fig. 33

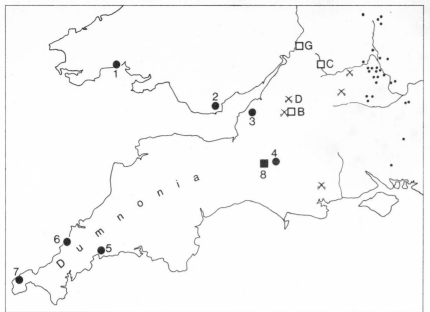

*32 The background to Cadbury-Camelot. The Badon campaign: 1–8 defended sites occupied, on the evidence of pottery, around AD 500: 1 Coygan, Carmarthenshire; 2 Dinas Powys, Glamorgan; 3 Cadbury-Congresbury, Somerset; 4 Cadbury-Camelot; 5 Castle Dore, Cornwall; 6 Trevelgue; 7 Chun Castle; 8 Ilchester, Somerset. The condition of the Roman town-walls of Ilchester about AD 500 is unknown, but the defences of Cadbury-Congresbury appear to have been derelict, leaving Cadbury-Camelot as the only known base for the defence of Dumnonia. ✕ suggested sites for Badon.
● Saxon settlement around AD 500 (after J. N. L. Myres,* Anglo-Saxon pottery and the settlement of England, *Oxford, 1969, map 8)*
The Dyrham campaign: B Bath; C Cirencester; D Dyrham; G Gloucester. By the time of Dyrham, there is evidence for Saxon penetration a little south and west of the earlier concentration

with their defences only slightly modified or re-furbished: only one is known to have undergone a major refortification comparable with Cadbury. Normally, the actual defences are far from impressive, though they may be enhanced, as at Castell Degannwy and Dinas Emrys, by a strong natural position. And all but one of them are quite small – less than a fifth of the area enclosed by the Cadbury defences. The exception, Cadbury-Congresbury, is a very complicated site, whose history is only now being unravelled by excavation. The Iron Age fort there encloses about half the acreage of Cadbury-Camelot, but the fifth-century enclosure is probably only half the size of its Iron Age precursor, and was apparently derelict by the time that our site was re-fortified.[73]

It is clear that the smallness of these forts of the late fifth and sixth centuries is directly related to the contemporary military organization. By the time that the pottery imports begin, those western and northern regions of Britain in which they are found were certainly under the politico-military

183

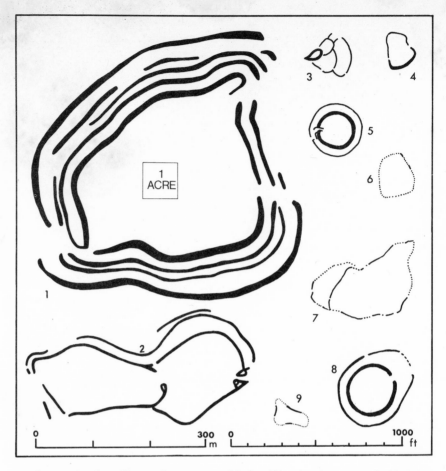

33 Comparative plans of forts producing pottery of the late fifth and sixth centuries; the fortifications were not necessarily defensible at that date. 1 Cadbury-Camelot; 2 Cadbury-Congresbury; 3 Dunadd, Argyll, capital of Scottic Dalriada; 4 Dinas Powys; 5 Chun Castle; 6 Castell Degannwy, Caernarvonshire, fortress of the princes of north-west Wales; 7 Dinas Emrys, Caernarvons.; 8 Castle Dore; 9 Mote of Mark, Kircudbrightshire

control of petty princes; and even the more Romanized lowlands were politically fragmented under the rule of *tyranni* or usurpers. The armed force appropriate to such rulers was the personal war-band or bodyguard: *comitatus* in Latin; *teulu*, 'family' in Welsh; *heorð-geneatas*, 'hearth-companions' in contemporary Anglo-Saxon society. It is difficult to suggest precise figures for the size of such armies. For an exceptional enterprise, the British attempt to overthrow the Anglian kingdom of Deira, an army of three hundred was gathered together. But for the war-band of a petty prince, something of the order of a hundred might be reasonable. And for such a force, the small fortifications which we know – the defended courts of princes – would be entirely appropriate.[74] But it seems ridiculous to

82 The first evidence of the Arthurian-period hall: Site L in 1968 (pp. 74–5). In addition to the usual Iron Age storage pits, and a shallow field ditch running up from left to right, there is a narrow but steep-sided wall-trench, running up from right to left. This contained fragments of a late-fifth or sixth-century wine-jar. Further exploration showed that the wall-trench had held a light screen or partition within the hall

83 The Arthurian-period hall (*Fig. 10, 15*), as uncovered in 1969, looking east (pp. 78–9, 177–8). White pegs stand in the post-holes attributed to the hall. For a plan and reconstruction see *Fig. 30*; compare also Plate 84

84 Looking west along the length of the Arthurian-period hall. White pegs stand in the post-holes of the hall; the wall-trench discovered in 1968 is immediately behind the second two-metre pole. This view gives a good impression of the commanding position of the hall on the highest part of the summit plateau. Compare Plate 83

85 The parallel wall-trenches of a small rectangular building (*Fig. 10*, 16) which may have been ancillary to the Arthurian-period hall. The white pegs in the right background mark the north-east corner of the hall

86 The mortared wall of Ethelredan Cadanbyrig as it was first discovered in 1966 (p. 49). The wall has a front face of well-laid lias slabs, backed by a rubble core. Behind this again, but not seen in this view, is a rear face (compare Plate 73). Behind the mortared wall is a wide earthen bank (p. 198)

87 The south-west gate of Cadanbyrig. In the foreground are the shattered remains of the left-hand respond or pier of the gate-arch, with Ham stone slabs protruding from the corner. To the right is the wall of the entrance passage (compare Plate 89), while to the left the front face of the *burh* wall is starting to rise up the hill (p. 198, *Fig. 35*). The Arthurian-period walling is just appearing in the background; compare Plate 76

88 Looking down the passage-way of the Ethelredan gate. It is likely that the passage had originally been paved with stone slabs, but if so these had been removed along with most of the walling, probably when the *burh* was abandoned by Cnut (*Gig. 35*; pp. 70, 201). As it reaches the excavation fence, the line of the passage does not run straight ahead, but turns very sharply to the right.

90 The eastern and southern arms of the cruciform trench (*Fig. 10, 29*) discovered on Site E in 1967 (p. 72). It seems likely that the trench had been dug for the foundations of a centrally-planned church (*Fig. 36*); but the actual constructional work had not been started when Ethelred lost control of the area, and the scheme was abandoned under Cnut (pp. 198–9). The bevelled re-entrant between the two arms of the cross is very clear. For plans see *Figs 8* and *36*

< 89 Looking across the Ethelredan passage to the best preserved length of walling. The Ham stone slab at the base of the front gate-arch can be seen at the point where the wall turns to run up the hill. Just to its right is another Ham slab with a socket for the gate pivot. Slight traces of the Arthurian-period wall can be seen protruding beneath the Ethelredan wall opposite the mid-point of the two-metre pole (*Fig. 35*)

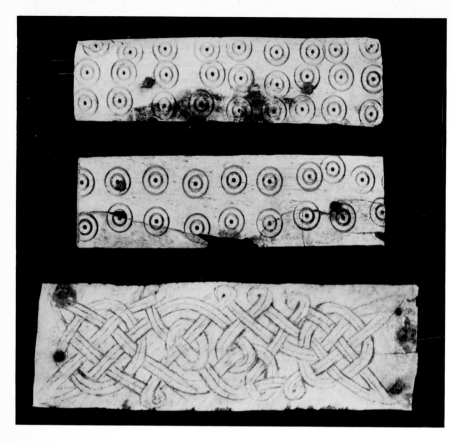

91 Late Saxon ornamental plaques of bone probably from a wooden casket. The largest piece, $4\frac{3}{8}$ ins long, is decorated in the Anglo-Saxon and Viking style of the early eleventh century

92 Iron knives, a chisel, and a buckle of Arthurian or Ethelredan date. The two left-hand knives are certainly fifth or sixth century; the other two knives could be either of that date or Late Saxon; and the chisel and buckle are almost certainly eleventh century. Actual size

93, 94 Post-Ethelredan walling at the south-west gate (pp. 69, 202–3). Massive blocks of yellow sandstone as they first appeared, and as they were subsequently uncovered overlying the mortared lias walling of the Ethelredan *burh*. There is no satisfactory historical explanation for this late phase

95 Field ditch of medieval or later date (*Fig. 10, 3*). This particular ditch which runs diagonally across the entire excavated area is seen here on Site B. Similar ditches were uncovered elsewhere on the same general alignment (*Fig. 10,* 1 and 2), and on Site EFG parallel plough scratches were visible in the bedrock (*Fig. 8*). These ditches are also parallel with the ridge and furrow visible on the earliest air-photograph of Cadbury Castle, taken in 1928. This suggests that this phase of agriculture is recent rather than medieval. It may even represent an extension of ploughing during the Napoleonic wars (pp. 203–4)

suggest such a role for Cadbury, with its twelve hundred yards of perimeter, and its eighteen-acre enclosure. And here two points deserve emphasis. First, the existence of Rampart E was proved on all sides of the site, in rampart cuttings A, D, I, J and K. Secondly, it had evidently been a deliberate act of policy to build a defensive work of this size. The shape of the Cadbury hill-top lends itself to the construction of a much smaller fort, something of the order of Castle Dore or Dinas Emrys, enclosing just the summit plateau and making use of the south-western scarp. Instead, some late fifth-century commander decided to fortify eighteen acres. Presumably he had a large garrison to accommodate, and a large labour force to carry out the work.

Cadbury and Arthur

It is here that the archaeological facts about Cadbury and the historical inferences about Arthur come together with the symbolism of Camelot. It is true, of course, that no personal relic of Arthur was found during the excavations – but the Camelot Research Committee had emphasized from the start that none was to be expected. This is in the nature of archaeological evidence. No personal tokens of the emperor Hadrian have ever been recovered from Hadrian's Wall, nor has any Edwardian castle produced a memento of Edward I. The historical evidence is that Arthur was not himself the ruler or war-leader of a single kingdom, but that he was 'leader of battles', *dux bellorum*, on behalf of several kingdoms. In this he appears as direct successor to Ambrosius Aurelianus, who led British resistance to the Anglo-Saxon settlers in the middle decades of the fifth century, and who probably commanded the forces of several *tyranni* owing a general allegiance to an overlord or high king.

We have no direct evidence for the size of the combined forces which Ambrosius and Arthur commanded, but we can make a controlled estimate. The lower limit is given by the three-hundred-strong army of the Gododdin, setting out from Edinburgh against Anglian Deira and perishing almost to a man at the battle of Catraeth, Catterick Bridge. The upper limit is set by the Roman field army in Britain about A D 400: not more than six thousand men, according to the best calculations. It is unthinkable that even the combined forces of several British successor kingdoms could match this figure. A thousand men might seem right for the armies of Ambrosius and Arthur. And Cadbury itself would be a suitable base for such a body.

There is, of course, no reason to connect Cadbury with the campaigns waged by Ambrosius. There is historical evidence that he was already an

Fig. 32

eminent soldier by AD 437, so he had probably retired before Cadbury was refortified in the 470s or later. But this date would fit Arthur, especially if we put his victory at Badon in AD 490 or 499. Just as the late sixth-century repair of the defences provided a base for the campaigns which had their climax in the British defeat at Deorham, so their original construction, a century earlier, could have provided a base for the campaigns which had their culmination in the British victory at Badon. The site of Badon itself is unknown, though the case for identifying it as Bath seems stronger than that for Badbury Rings, Dorset, or Badbury near Liddington Castle in Wiltshire.[75] There is at least agreement that it was fought against the Anglo-Saxons in southern England. And it is worth remembering here that, although the recorded history of Wessex begins with the founders of the dynasty, Cerdic and Cynric, landing from Southampton Water in AD 495, the archaeological evidence is for a vigorous settlement in the Upper Thames valley from the 450s.[76]

These are speculations only; but in a period in which facts are so few, some speculation is both legitimate and necessary. The minimal facts may usefully be recapitulated. Arthur was a great warrior, concerned especially with campaigns against the Saxon settlers around AD 500. On present evidence, Cadbury was outstanding at this time among British fortresses in terms of the size and strength of its defences. Whether Arthur was personally connected with it or not, it illustrates the kind of defended base which he might have used. With every justification, we can think of Arthur and his troops feasting and carousing – like the Gododdin army in the hall of Myddynog Mwynfawr – in a hall similar to that at Cadbury; and riding out to battle through a gate-tower like that at the south-west entrance.

Saxons and Vikings in Wessex

After the victory of Dyrham, eastern Dumnonia did not immediately fall into Saxon hands. A battle at Beandun, perhaps Bindon in east Devon, in 614, shows the Saxon kingdom of Wessex probing along the south coast, but it was not until 658 that the *Wealas*, the Welsh or Britons, were driven back to the river Parrett. No evidence is available to show what part Cadbury might have played in seventh-century campaigns. Once the rule of Wessex was asserted over Somerset, it would certainly have been abandoned, for the Saxons at that time had no interest in fortified hill-tops. So the fort lay derelict until the emergencies of Ethelred's reign gave a new urgency to the need for strong defences.

Ethelred II, Æthelræd Unræd, 'Noble-counsel No-counsel' or 'Noble-counsel Evil-counsel', came to the throne of Wessex in 978. Almost two centuries earlier, the *Anglo-Saxon Chronicle* records the first Viking assault on Wessex. Through the ninth and early tenth centuries, Viking raids on England had passed into settlement, and the settlement itself had been contained by the kings of Wessex, Alfred and his successors. At the time of Ethelred's accession, England had enjoyed a long respite from raiding; but two years later, the peace was broken by the appearance of fresh Viking forces at Southampton, in Thanet, and in Cheshire. These new raiders were altogether more formidable than the old, a permanent professional fleet and army rather than bands of adventurers. Their activities were recorded contemporaneously in minute and circumstantial detail in the *Anglo-Saxon Chronicle*.[77] From that record I propose to extract only the events which are immediately relevant to Cadbury. The first of these was the appearance of the fleet and army of Thorkell the Tall in August 1009. From then until 1012 Thorkell's army 'harried and burned as was their wont' in southern and eastern England, and as far north as Northampton, as far west as the vale of Pewsey.[78] Meanwhile, in September 1009 or March 1010, Ethelred had founded the emergency *burh* of Cadanbyrig.

The Late Saxon *burh* or fortified town was essentially a military device developed by Alfred and his successors in order to defend Wessex and to consolidate their hold on territory as they won it back from the Danes. Elaborate arrangements to maintain the defences and their garrisons demonstrate the administrative sophistication of Late Saxon England. Normally the *burh* was low-lying, involving either the defence of a pre-existing centre of population and commerce, or the foundation of a new one. Two exceptions, the refortified Iron Age forts of Cadbury and of Cissbury in Sussex, are both works of Ethelred's reign, and reflect the seriousness of the emergency in the early eleventh century. The actual defences of early *burhs* were of earth, with timber palisades or breastworks. But in AD 917, a *burh* which had been built in this way at Towcester before Easter was strengthened with a stone wall in the autumn. From that time on, any newly-founded *burh* would have been fortified with a masonry wall, and similar walls were added to existing *burhs*.[79]

Apart from their defensive functions, the *burhs* were commercial and administrative centres. As one aspect of this, many of them contained royal mints, for a strictly controlled currency was another mark of Late Saxon administrative efficiency. The normal coin was a silver penny, which bore on the obverse the name of the ruler with a crude portrait; and on the reverse,

Fig. 34

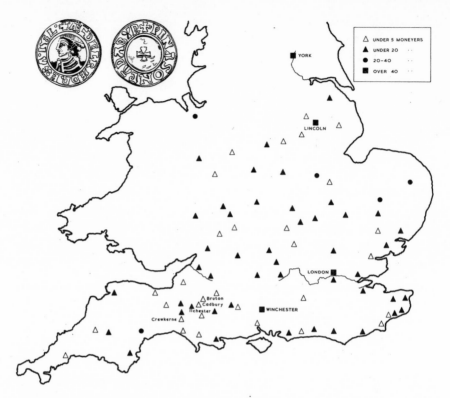

34 Mints in operation at varying times during Ethelred's reign (AD 978–1016), with the numbers of the moneyers operating at them. The silver penny shown above (actual size) was struck at Ethelredan Cadanbyrig by the moneyer Winas

the name of the moneyer and of the mint town, surrounding a symbolic design, frequently a cross. Thus a typical penny from the Cadbury mint reads:

+ EDELREDREX.A.NGL. + WINASONCADABYR

    Ethelred King of the English   Winas at Cadbury

What the coins lack is any *anno domini* date of minting. The date can, however, be inferred: broadly, from the historically-known dates of the rulers; more narrowly from the typological development within each reign; most precisely, because the type itself was changed periodically, and all the existing coins were then re-called.[80]

    The Cadanbyrig mint was founded by a group of moneyers who had previously been minting at the lowland *burh* of Ilchester, some seven miles to the west. The abandonment of Ilchester and the founding of the Cadanbyrig mint coincided with a change of type which numismatists date to either September 1009 or March 1010. It is clear that the move was an emergency measure, intended to remove one mint at least to a place of safety. But this poses the question, was the mint set up in a pre-existing Late

Fig. 34

Saxon fort; or were *burh* and mint simultaneous foundations? There is in fact no evidence for a *burh* at Cadanbyrig independent of the mint, and a hill-top town would be most unlikely under normal Late Saxon conditions. The two must therefore go together. And if the creation of the mint dates the foundation of the *burh*, its removal should likewise date the abandonment. Under Ethelred's successor, Cnut, the original Ilchester moneyers moved back there. A few coins of Cnut's early issues were in fact struck at Cadanbyrig, but the moneyers responsible appear shortly afterwards at Crewkerne and Bruton. The numismatic evidence gives the limits of 1009 to 1019 for the *burh* and mint of Cadanbyrig.[81]

This has taken us beyond the appearance of Thorkell the Tall, and we must now return to the last years of Ethelred's reign. In 1013 the whole character of the struggle was changed when Swein Forkbeard, the Danish ruler, came to England with the intention of taking over the kingdom. District after district submitted to him, while Ethelred himself retired first to his fleet in the Thames, and then to Normandy. By the end of 1013 Swein was regarded as king by most of the country, but his death in February 1014 threw the situation once more into flux. Over the next two and a half years, there was a struggle for power between Ethelred, his son Edmund Ironside, and Swein's son Cnut, which was only finally resolved by the deaths of Ethelred and Edmund in April and November 1016 respectively. From the end of 1016, Cnut was undisputed master of England, and it was possible to re-establish firm and orderly government. But during the years of turmoil, Wessex had been now in the hands of Cnut, now of Edmund Ironside. This is the political background to Cadanbyrig.

The archaeology of Cadanbyrig

The first thing to be said about Cadanbyrig is that no trace of the mint was located during the excavations. This is not surprising: when the moneyers returned to Ilchester, or went to Crewkerne and Bruton, they would obviously have taken their dies and other tools with them, and they would certainly not have abandoned ingots of silver. But if the mint was not found, there was good evidence for the *burh* defences. As with earlier works, these involved the refortification of twelve hundred yards of perimeter. In this case, we can calculate the appropriate size for the garrison. An early tenth-century document, the *Burghal Hidage*, shows that four men were needed to man each pole (five and a half yards) of wall. This gives a paper garrison of about 870 men for Cadanbyrig.[82]

Fig. 4

Plates 73, 86

The main feature of the defences was a mortared stone wall, four feet wide. Where the face of this was preserved, for instance in Cut A, it consisted of beautifully laid Lias slabs, specially imported for their quality as building stone. Behind this was a rubble core of local rock, bound with a rather soft mortar. This in turn was backed with a bank of earth, rubble, and even large boulders – whatever came most readily to hand – to an overall width of twenty feet. Only in one place, in part of Cutting D, was any evidence found for a rear wall of mortared stone. There is no evidence to suggest that this was related to some special feature such as a tower. The implication is that it had been intended to face the inside of the bank with masonry all round the perimeter, but the work had never been completed. It should be added that we have no evidence for the original height of either the bank or the wall, but it is reasonable to think that the wall was carried up as a parapet protecting a wall-walk.

Plates 87–89

Fig. 35

The south-west gateway through the defences was explored, as far as its ruined condition allowed, in 1968 and 1969. The main feature was a simple passage-way about ten feet wide by thirty feet or more long. This was walled in well-laid Lias, set in a hard white mortar. We do not know how the passage was roofed. A flat wooden ceiling is possible, but a barrel vault might be more appropriate to the quality of the masonry. The outer end of the passage was narrowed with piers or responds carried up in Ham stone, imported from ten miles away. The doorway itself may have had a flat lintel, or an arch turned in Ham stone. The known quality of Late Saxon churches in the area, for instance at Milborne Port, assures us that the gates of Cadanbyrig could have been accomplished works of architecture. The door itself was probably double-leaved, and had turned on sockets cut in Ham stone slabs, one of which was found almost in its original position in the passage.

Plates 9, 90

One other structure may be attributed to the Ethelredan *burh*: the cruciform trench on Site E. This is a rock-cut trench, normally about five feet wide, varying in depth from four to twenty inches, marking out a regular equal-armed cross one hundred and thirty feet overall. One other feature of the plan deserves notice: the re-entrants between the four arms of the cross are not right-angled, but deliberately bevelled. The trench cuts several Iron Age pits, and its filling contains weathered sherds of Ultimate Iron Age pottery, so it must date to the very end of the Iron Age or later. The filling itself, of soil and small stones, is completely uninformative. These are the observed facts; from this point we must either preserve a despairing silence, or speculate.

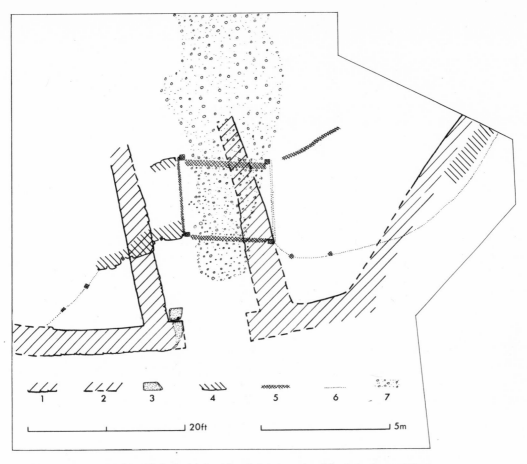

35 *The south-west gate of the Ethelredan burh with underlying remains of the Arthurian-period gate. 1 Ethelredan mortared wall with face preserved; 2 Ethelredan wall with facing lost; 3 Ham stone piers for arch and slab with socket for gate-pivot; 4 Arthurian-period dry-stone walling; 5 traces of timber beams and posts; 6 Arthurian-period structures, inferred; 7 late sixth-century repair to roadway*

Fig. 36

In 1968, I put forward a closely-argued case for regarding this as the foundation trench for a Late Saxon church which had never actually been built; and I also published a conjectural reconstruction of the kind of church which might have been intended.[83] No reasoned refutation of my case has appeared in print, and no alternative suggestion has been put forward, so my hypothesis stands. Only the briefest outline of the case can be repeated here. The trench was dug for the foundations of a masonry structure consisting of a central square which projected into the bevelled re-entrants, and four smaller square units. Such a structure recalls centrally-planned churches, and no other known form of building. The orientation, thirty degrees north of east, is within the range of medieval churches. The projection of the central feature can be paralleled in several Late Saxon churches where the tower is wider than chancel, nave, and transepts. The absence of mortar from the

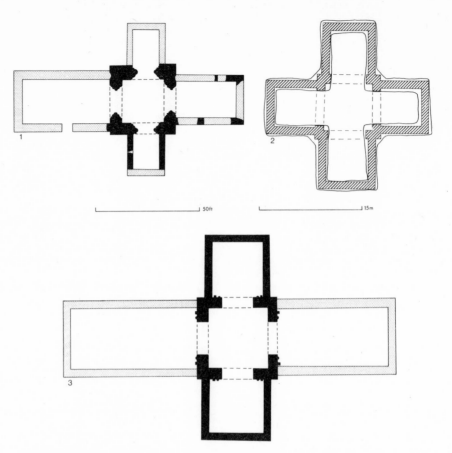

36 *Three Late Saxon churches with square towers projecting in the angles between the nave, chancel and transepts. 1 Milborne Port, Somerset; 2 Cadanbyrig; walling inferred from the foundation trench uncovered in 1967–69; 3 Stow, Lincolnshire. (Milborne Port and Stow after H. M. and J. Taylor, Anglo-Saxon architecture, Cambridge, 1965.)*

trench shows that the church had never been built. The very brief history of the *burh* provides an acceptable context for a building which was planned, had its foundations dug, and was then abandoned. The overall bracket is AD 1009–1019, but the disturbed state of Wessex from 1013 to 1017 makes it doubtful whether any serious building could have been undertaken in those years.

The finds from this short-lived *burh* are naturally sparse, but nonetheless varied. Unfortunately no silver pennies were found, but this is perhaps not surprising when we consider how much of the currency minted for Ethelred went straight into Viking coffers as loot and bribes. A number of hard-fired, coarsely gritted cooking pots must be Late Saxon, rather than later. Several iron knives with a long thick back are characteristic of Viking and Late Saxon England. But the most interesting pieces from Ethelred's *burh* are some ornamental strips of bone from a wooden casket. Most of them

Plate XI
Plates 91, 92

have very simple decoration, but one has the elaborate interlace typical of
the period. Clearly, some of the arts could still flourish amid the march and
countermarch of English and Viking armies.

We have seen that the Cadbury mint stopped production early in Cnut's
reign, and it is reasonable to think that Cadanbyrig, an inconvenient hill-top
town, was then abandoned. But the archaeological evidence allows us to go
further than this. Only in one of our rampart cuttings was the outer face of
the *burh* wall present. At the gate, three or four courses were still in place
along the left hand side of the passage, but on the right only a yard or so of
walling, three courses high, was preserved. This walling had not disappeared
through dereliction and collapse. No mortared stone was found tumbled
into Ditch 1; and at the gate, the walling had not collapsed across the passage-
way. Indeed, the paving of the passage had itself vanished. The evidence
points conclusively to a systematic demolition of defences and gates. There
can be no doubt that this was done on the orders of Cnut, who could not
leave a fortress standing empty as a potential base for English or Viking
rivals.

Plates 88, 89

IX After Cadanbyrig

Medieval Cadbury

Our archaeological information does not come to an abrupt stop after Cnut's demolition of Cadanbyrig, though the scraps which remain form a poor tail-piece to the main Cadbury story. First of all, the south-west gate was rebuilt on top of the Ethelredan ruins. The re-build was in dry stone-work, using a mixture of very massive blocks of yellow sandstone and some Lias slabs. It had been badly mutilated, probably by farmers digging out the stones in later centuries, so that only part of the outer end of the passage had been preserved. The entrance itself was ten feet wide, but there was no trace of gate- or door-arrangements. Rather similar dry stone walling, using large yellow blocks, is recognizable in the defence cuttings all round the perimeter. In 1966 we thought that this was a rear wall for the Late Saxon bank, but a closer study of the stratification showed that it was in fact later, and had been cut into the back of the Ethelredan rampart. The stratification, as well as the character of the stonework, relates it to the re-build at the gate. In other words, we have here evidence for a crude but comprehensive re-walling of the hill-top.

It is uncertain, however, whether we can reasonably call the yellow wall and gate a refortification. The gate is not at all military in character. The fact that round the perimeter the wall is on the inside, not the outside of the bank suggests that it was intended to keep something in the fort rather than to keep enemies out. It seems likely that the yellow wall and gate were intended to turn the fort into a large stock enclosure, but we have no evidence when this was done.

There is, however, a hint of medieval military activity at Cadbury. In 1209, a sum of forty marks (£12.16.4 or £12.82) was paid from King John's household accounts *ad opera castri de Cadebir*, 'towards building work at the castle of Cadbury'. There is no other reference either to the castle or to the *opera*, and it is even in dispute which Cadbury is intended. The fact

Plate 73

that the recipients of the money, Peter de Scudamore and Godfrey de St Martin, were active in Wiltshire and Dorset about this time creates a slight bias in favour of our Cadbury. The identification is clinched, as tightly as the character of the evidence will allow, by discoveries on Site M in 1968. It was shown that the scarp at the south-western end of the summit plateau had been artificially steepened. More important, above the scarp was a square-sectioned trench, dug into the solid rock of the hill to a depth of two feet and a width of eight feet, and obviously intended as the foundation trench for a masonry wall. From its floor came a large part of a twelfth- or early thirteenth-century cooking pot. This, then, could be part of the *opera*: a castle projected, but never completed, on the strongest part of the hill. Two leading students of the historical sources have drily remarked that it is not clear why John should have chosen to embark on such a project.[84]

For the rest, the history of Cadbury is agricultural, antiquarian, and archaeological. Outside the defences, especially on the south, less clearly on the east and north-east, is a series of terraces, known locally as 'The Linches'. Their purpose is, of course, not military, but agricultural, to make possible the plough-cultivation of a steep slope, and perhaps also to increase the actual surface area available for grazing. It is almost certain that they are deliberately built, rather than an accidental by-product of ploughing along the slope. Similar 'strip lynchets' are widely known on the slopes of the Wessex downs and elsewhere in southern England, and there has been a great deal of controversy about their date of construction and period of use. Two of the Cadbury lynchets appear quite clearly in Stukeley's 'Prospect of Camalet Castle', already overlaid by a well-developed hedge. So here at least the lynchets had been abandoned as part of a system of land-holding and cultivation by the early eighteenth century. On the other hand, Bennett tells us that those on the south of the hill had been cultivated within his memory.

Later cultivation of the hill-top itself has also left archaeological traces. One of the clearest of the patterns on the geophysical plots is a series of linear anomalies running roughly south-west to north-east across the hill. In 1967 we hoped that some of these marked the parallel wall-trenches of rectangular buildings of Arthurian or Ethelredan date. Excavation showed, however, that they were actually indicating shallow, featureless ditches. An obvious explanation was that these ditches, and the banks of spoil which must originally have stood beside them, marked field boundaries for some kind of strip field. In confirmation of this agricultural interpretation, on Site E F G shallow grooves could still be seen in the rock running parallel with

Fig. 5

Plate 1

Fig. 3

Plate 2

Plates 9, 95

Figs. 8, 10

one of the ditches. These were certainly plough scratches. The fact that they had not disappeared through the weathering of the soft rock argued for their being recent. As it happens, the earliest known air-photograph of Cadbury, taken by the Royal Air Force in January 1928, shows the hill-top ploughed in ridges which run parallel with some of the ditches. So air-photography and archaeology complement one another with evidence about a system of agriculture which, from unknown beginnings, lasted well into the present century.

Finally, some account should be given of the traces of walling which are still visible on the hill-top today. The clearest stretch is to be seen just to the left as one comes in through the South Cadbury or north-east entrance, where the inner face of the bank is revetted with well-laid blocks of dry-stonework. Comparable walling surrounds the whole perimeter, but in some places it has either collapsed or has grassed over. At the south-west entrance, this walling over-rides all phases of the gate, and passes out through the entrance passage to the foot of the hill. In 1890, Bennett claimed that the wall was at least two hundred and fifty years old, but he quotes no authority for his statement. Since it is not mentioned by Stukeley in his detailed account, it is almost certain that it was not in existence at the time of his visit in 1723. It is most likely to be a product of late eighteenth- or nineteenth-century farming, intended to allow cattle to graze the banks while keeping them out of the cornlands of the interior. Whatever its date and purpose, it is disturbing that this wall has deteriorated quite markedly within living memory.

After the excavations

I have now taken my account of the history of Cadbury up to the point where archaeologists, Bennett, St George Gray, and ultimately the Camelot Research Committee, began their investigations: we have come full circle back to the beginning. But in Part One I deliberately omitted certain aspects of the recent excavations, simply because they seemed more appropriate to the end of the book than to its middle. These matters can be summed up in a single question, often asked by laymen: 'What happens now to the site and the finds?' To this enquiry, and others like it, the archaeologist has a set of stock answers. Whether or not they are satisfactory is another matter.

The chief question the layman really wants to ask is 'Why ever did you stop digging, when you've only excavated about six per cent of the site?' For the Arthurian enthusiast this challenge is given teeth by my own admission that just inside the south-west gate there is a major focus of Arthurian-period activity which we omitted to excavate.

The first reason why, on any large archaeological site, the digging eventually has to stop is that there is a limit to the resources of money and skilled man-power which are available. The learned societies and public bodies which provide the hard core of finance will make large grants for a finite project, but not for one which is open-ended. They rallied to our 1970 season with generous support because the Committee had firmly declared that this was to be the final year of excavation.

Moreover, by 1970 the Cadbury team itself was breaking up, for reasons which are worth explaining. It might be thought that on such a large project the senior members of the team – the Director and his Deputy, the Finds Supervisor and the Site Supervisors – would be permanent, salaried officers. Nothing could be further from the case. The Director was a full-time university teacher, the principal supervisors were full-time undergraduate and graduate students, and for all of us, Cadbury was a spare-time activity. As supervisors came to the end of their university courses, they necessarily had to seek paid employment, which normally left them without the leisure to commit themselves to a long excavating season. This was no doubt very unsatisfactory, but it happens to be the current state of affairs in the organization of British archaeology.

Another practical limit was imposed in South Cadbury itself. It is probable that the hamlet could have absorbed the excavation and the diggers, at the cost of minor tensions in the village pub where diggers sometimes swamped out the locals. But what South Cadbury could not absorb was our visitors, in their coach-loads and in cars by the thousand. In this respect local tolerance and patience were not inexhaustible; and by the end of 1970, they were nearly bankrupt.

There were also issues of principle. Any excavation must be seen in wider perspectives of archaeological research. It may be regrettable that only six per cent of the interior of Cadbury has been examined. On the other hand, no other major English hillfort has been excavated as extensively as Cadbury, or in accordance with a similar policy of research. What is now needed is work on a dozen hillforts, on the same scale as that at Cadbury, and perhaps governed by a comparable policy, but directed by men with interests and prejudices different from my own.

Moreover, there is a good case for leaving important features of any one site undisturbed so that future generations may investigate them. Just as St George Gray's excavations were more advanced technically than Bennett's, and mine than Gray's, so thirty years hence someone with greater technical resources and more developed skills than my own will wish to excavate that focus of Arthurian-period activity by the south-west gate. I hope that I may be there to see the results.

There is a further, even more important reason for bringing the digging to a halt: the need to study and to publish our discoveries. There would, after all, have been no point in digging if all the objects we found, all the plans of buildings, all the photographs of ramparts were simply to be locked away in cupboards or buried in a basement at University College, Cardiff. Publication, when all is said and done, is the ultimate purpose of excavation – though one might not guess this from the activity of some archaeologists. And the necessary prelude to publication is a very detailed study of all our finds, in relation to the ramparts and buildings at Cadbury, and in comparison with similar objects from other sites. It is true, of course, that everything was inspected as it came out of the ground, but only a cursory examination was possible during the excavation itself. In brief, the digging had to stop so that the proper study of our discoveries might begin.

The second question which the layman asks is 'Why do you fill all the trenches in and cover everything up?' This comes especially from local people, who had hoped that the walling of the Ethelredan gate, so splendid in appearance, might remain uncovered for future generations to see. In this case, the answer is plain. We ourselves had to remove every stone of the Ethelredan gate so that we could explore the Arthurian and Iron Age gates buried beneath it. Even if this had not been necessary, it would still not have been possible to leave the Ethelredan walling exposed. Both mortar and stonework had perished after nine hundred years of burial, and a few winters' frosts would soon have destroyed what had been left by King Cnut. As for the interior of the site, nothing could be left open there, because pits, gullies and post-holes would rapidly have silted up with wind-blown dust, their sides would have crumbled with frost, and weeds would have sprung up on the rock between them.

Beyond this, there is usually an obligation on the archaeologist, when he has finished digging, to restore a site to its original appearance, and to return the land to its normal use. No one would quarrel with the first point: the last thing we want is that our ancient monuments should be left with the gaping wounds of excavators' trenches. The second point is more debatable. The man-in-the-street with a taste for history and archaeology might imagine that our ancient hillforts and other sites belong first and foremost to the nation – this is what 'national heritage' means. As part of our common history, they should be readily available for examination by suitably skilled researchers; and they should be freely open to the visits of the ordinary citizen. This should be especially true in the case of sites like Cadbury, whose outstanding interest has been demonstrated by excavation.

The actual position is very different. However important a monument might seem, it belongs not to the nation, but to the person on whose land it stands; and he has almost absolute power over it. Unless there are established rights of way, the public has no claim to access: at Cadbury this is limited to a footpath round the defences. Archaeologists can claim no right to inspect, still less to survey or to excavate a monument: the whole Cadbury operation was dependent on the enlightenment and goodwill of Mr and Mrs Montgomery, the owners. Finally, even when a site is nominally protected as a 'scheduled monument' under the Ancient Monuments Act, the landowner may obliterate it by ploughing, afforestation, quarrying, building, or in any other way he wishes – provided he gives three months notice to the Department of the Environment. So much for the national heritage! In face of this, the obligation to return farming land to its original use after excavation must seem rather mild.

The landowner's rights over the finds from an excavation are also absolute. Unless objects are declared Treasure Trove, they belong to the landowner, who may legally sell them – to foreigners if he wishes; keep a few pretty things for himself and throw the rest away; give them all to his friends; or deposit some or all of them in a museum. For an object to be Treasure Trove, it must not only be of precious metal, like our gold Covesea bracelet, or the gold coin of Antethos; it must also be proved that the original owner had deposited it, as he thought, in a safe place, intending to recover it. It then belongs to the Crown, but the finder (not the landowner) is paid the market value of the piece. None of the objects from Cadbury was proved to be Treasure Trove, and everything therefore belongs to the landowners. Fortunately the owners of Cadbury have decided to place the great bulk of the finds in the Somerset County Museum at Taunton, where they will join the material from St George Gray's excavation and from Mrs Harfield's collection.

Before this can happen, however, there is much to be done to the finds. The treatment varies: at one extreme are featureless scraps of pottery, which require a quick examination with a hand lens before they become a figure in a statistical table; at the other are frail and priceless bronzes, like the face plaque from the gate, or the shield-mount from the plateau, which have required months of the most skilled treatment in the laboratory of the

British Museum. All objects are cleaned, and if necessary they are strengthened with plastic resins. All are examined, classified and tabulated, and those which merit it are drawn and photographed as well.

Part of this treatment is necessary in order to preserve objects which have lain for hundreds or thousands of years in a stable environment in the ground, so that they do not corrode or disintegrate when exposed to the atmosphere. But the main work of classifying, illustrating and cataloguing the objects is in preparation for the full and final report on the excavations. Interlocked, therefore, with the research on the objects is that on the structures where they were found.

On countless photographs, plans and other drawings the evidence for defences, gates and buildings must be analysed, and correlated with other structures at Cadbury, and with similar structures on other sites. Then paper reconstructions must be attempted, firstly of particular buildings, individual pots and so on; then of entire cultural phases; and finally, the whole history of Cadbury must be reconstructed in the imagination.

Obviously this has already been done in outline, or the present book could not have been written. The layman may well ask 'How will the final report differ from the book; and why should it be different?' To take the second question first. When a scientific discovery is reported, it is usually sufficient to state the hypothesis that is being tested, to describe the apparatus and the procedures used, and to give the result of the experiment. Any other scientist can then build similar apparatus, repeat the procedure, and obtain the same result, thereby verifying the experiment. But no one who wishes to verify my observations and test my hypotheses will ever be able to repeat the procedure which I used at the south-west gate. The evidence no longer exists at Cadbury – it was totally destroyed in' the digging. The only clues that remain lie in eight ring-back binders, five rolls of drawings, some hundreds of photo-negatives and transparencies, and a score of cardboard boxes of pottery and other objects.

The historian studies his document, and returns it to the safe-keeping of a library; the scientist's experiment is repeated in other laboratories; but the archaeologist's experiment is unrepeatable because he has destroyed the primary evidence. Consequently, he has an absolute obligation to publish, as fully as possible, the records which he made during the excavation. This gives his colleagues some opportunity of judging whether his methods of excavating were sound, and whether his observations were acute, and therefore likely to be reliable. From this they can proceed to judge the plausibility of his hypotheses. Conversely (or perversely) they may decide that quite different hypotheses will explain the evidence more reasonably. This is only possible if it is presented very fully and fairly.

All this, of course, determines the character of the final report. In comparison with this book, it will be enormously, even tediously, detailed, both in words and illustrations. Much of it will consist of lists, tables and catalogues. Its language will be technical, and its statements will be qualified. Whereas here I have stated the most likely explanations, in the full report I will have to argue a case, stating and rejecting unlikely hypotheses, before settling for the best one. Lastly, where this book presents the Director's own interpretation, in the final report part of my role will be to edit detailed specialist reports written by experts in particular fields.

Two points should have emerged from all this. Firstly, the work of excavating Cadbury is at an end, for this generation at least. Secondly, the detailed research goes on: less spectacular than the digging, but no less arduous. And in the long run, it is this research, and the publication which results from it, which bring the digging itself to its true fulfilment.

Chronological Table

DATE	PERIOD	DEFENCES	S W GATE	INTERIOR
4000	NEO-LITHIC — EARLY			
3000	Field bank?		Ritual pits
	LATE			
2000	BRONZE AGE — EARLY			
1000	MIDDLE	Ditch, K618		
900	LATE	No		
800		defences		
700		Turf forming		Cooking and other pits
600	INITIAL			
500	IRON AGE — EARLY	Rampart A		Six-post-houses?
400		Rampart B	Single guard-chamber	
300	MIDDLE			Round-
200		Rampart C several phases	Paired guard-chambers	houses
100	LATE	Outer banks added		
BC / AD	ULTIMATE	Rampart D	Single guard-chamber	Porched shrine
100			Massacre	Field-oven, barracks
200	ROMAN			
300				Romano-Celtic temple?
400				
500	ARTHURIAN	Rampart E	Gate-tower	Feasting hall
600			Tower refurbished	
700				
800				
900				
1000	ETHELREDAN	Masonry wall	Masonry gate	Church
1100				
1200		Castrum de Cadebir?	Yellow gate?	
1300				

FINDS	BACKGROUND EVENTS	DATE
	Windmill Hill culture First farmers	4000
Simple bowls, trumpet lugs Flint axes, leaf arrows		
		3000
Rinyo-Clacton bowl Bronze axe	Grooved-ware culture	2000
	Deverel-Rimbury culture	1000
	Urnfield cultures	
		900
		800
Covesea gold bracelet Bronze knives, spear Large plain jars	Hallstatt B	
		700
Bronze razors Neck-cordon jars	Hallstatt C	600
Swan's neck pins Jars with finger-tip ornament Fine bowls	Hallstatt D	500
		400
Simple jars		300
		200
Bead-rim jars Wide-range of decorated pottery Iron currency bars and other metal work		100
Coins	58–51 Caesar's conquest of Gaul	BC
Wheel-thrown pottery		AD
Rare Roman pottery Military bronzes	43 Claudian invasion of Britain	100
		200
Late Roman coins Gilt bronze A		300
	406 Germanic barbarians cross Rhine	400
Imported bowls and amphorae	c. 500 Battle of Badon	500
	577 Battle of Dyrham	600
		700
	789 First recorded Viking attack on Wessex	800
		900
	978 Ethelred the Unready	1000
Late Saxon pottery, bone and metal	1016 Cnut	
		1100
	1199 1216 John	1200
		1300

Epilogue

It seems fitting to end this account of the Cadbury-Camelot excavations with a brief evaluation of their significance, as it appears shortly after the end of the field-work and with the detailed analysis of finds and structures still far from complete. I begin with what the Press called 'The quest for Camelot'. We did not find the fabulous Camelot, nor add anything directly to historical knowledge about Arthur as a person. But at the least, the quest stimulated debate and research into Arthurian problems, both on the site and in wider academic circles. And even if the discussions sometimes generated coolness rather than light, our understanding of the historical Arthur, and of the situation in which he acted, has certainly been enriched.[85]

Beyond this, there have been solid and surprising gains in our knowledge of the material background of the Arthurian period. I would be the first to stress that in terms of minor artefacts, my excavations at Dinas Powys yielded more information for a twentieth the cost of the Cadbury dig.[86] But the possibility of building up a revolutionary account of economic and social aspects of the period on the basis of the Dinas Powys evidence was due simply to the fact that artefacts and documents had not previously been related together. At Cadbury, the solid results were the uncovering of a major defensive work; of a gate-tower which is the only one known in the period; and of a timber hall, one of the only three known. Because of the vastness of the site, and the depth of post-Arthurian overlay, these results could only be achieved at great expense. The surprise was the discovery of the hall, for while the location of the defences and the gate was obvious, there were no clues at all to its whereabouts. Before the excavation began, I made a crude estimate of the odds, based on the total area of the Cadbury fort in comparison with that of the hall at Castle Dore. As a result, I warned the Camelot Research Committee that our chances of locating a hall were two hundred to one against.

These major Arthurian discoveries will, in course of time, form an accepted part of our overall picture of a period which is at once fascinating and obscure. But because Arthurian Cadbury is only one phase in the long history of the site, the 'Quest for Camelot' had to take its place within a much broader programme of research. Some of the more important discoveries may be listed briefly. The Neolithic phases remained obstinately enigmatic, but for the Late Bronze Age we explored a small settlement, and made a major contribution to the study of the little-known pottery of the period. The transition from Bronze Age to Iron Age, a period of major importance in the peopling of these islands, was elucidated for one site. Associated and stratified groups of pottery and other objects were collected to provide firmer and richer evidence for the history of the Iron Age in west-southern England. New aspects of the Roman treatment of the native Britons were revealed. The only Late Saxon masonry gateway available for exploration anywhere in England was fully excavated. And among notable buildings, special mention might be made of the six-post Iron Age structures; the stake-built round house; the porched shrine of the Ultimate Iron Age; and the foundation-trench of the cruciform church.

The Iron Age merits further discussion, particularly in terms of the questions which I had posed before the excavations began. How far had our policy of excavation been successful in answering these questions? There is no doubt at all that, by concentrating on the interior rather than on the defences, and by exploring the central area rather than the periphery, we gained new insights into the status and function of Iron Age hillforts. Here is one fort at least which had been a focus both for ritual and for the highest levels of craftsmanship. Here too, by inference, was a seat of the aristocracy. But before we can start to generalize from Cadbury to other forts, we need more – I would say, many more – excavations directed in accordance with the same policy. Even then, we may not be able to answer questions about the density of population in hillforts.

Here I think that Cadbury has a warning to offer against premature generalization and synthesis. It is the most extensively excavated fort in Britain, and evidence for a very long cultural sequence has been amassed. But it has also emerged that every cultural phase except the Late Iron Age had its own very restricted distribution within the eighteen acres of the interior. I have already commented on the absence of pits of the Early phase of the Iron Age from the areas which we excavated, and I have suggested that the main focus of settlement (which we can suspect from pottery in the ramparts) lay elsewhere. A similar explanation seems to fit the distribution

213

of Arthurian artefacts. If we had dug other parts of the site we might have found the principal centres of the Early Iron Age and Arthurian occupations, but missed the Late Bronze Age or the early Roman phases. The one safe generalization here is that it is impossible, from a small sample, to generalize about the cultural history of a hillfort, let alone about its population, economy, status and function.

Despite this, we find respected scholars advocating limited excavations on the hillforts of an area in order to establish their culture, date and economy. As a historian with some interest in early medieval social and economic problems, I sometimes think that my prehistorian colleagues not only make bricks without clay, but then use them to build large straw edifices.

To return to Cadbury. We have now collected the primary evidence for a history of one hillfort. Some years of cataloguing and analysis lie ahead before that history can be written in circumstantial detail. But enough is already known to reveal the importance of Cadbury. A magnificent site by nature, with sweeping views and dramatic atmosphere, it was seized upon by early man as an ideal place for settlement. Nature was then improved with a series of defences which in their serried steepness can rival any hillfort in England. And through recurring times of strife, the hill and the defences were used again and again. So Cadbury came to outdo all other sites in the number and time span of its occupations. It was not the Arthurian period alone, but Cadbury's four thousand years of history that stimulated the interest from which this book takes its own inspiration.

Appendix

The Battle of Badon

We have two early accounts of the battle of Badon or Badonicus.[87] The western British monk Gildas wrote a potted history of Britain as a prelude to his lengthy denunciation of the sins of kings and bishops in his own day. He tells us how Anglo-Saxon mercenaries were employed to defend Britain; how they mutinied against their paymasters, and overran much of the land; and how Ambrosius rallied the Britons to victory.

'From then on' (continues Gildas) 'victories were won sometimes by our men, sometimes by the enemy, up to the time of the siege of mount Badonicus. That was almost the last slaughter of the thugs, but certainly not the least. It happened forty-three years and one month ago, as I well know, because it was at the time of my own birth.'

Our second account is found in a document commonly known as *Annales Cambriae*, but more exactly described as the British Easter Annals. This is a list of important events – the deaths of saints, bishops and kings, and major battles – which had been recorded as they occurred in the margin of a set of tables used for calculating, year by year, the date of Easter. Long afterwards, a twelfth-century historian had copied all the historical records out of the Easter Tables, thus producing the British Easter Annals. The entry about Badon runs as follows:

'Year 72. Battle of Badon in which Arthur carried the cross of our lord Jesus Christ three days and three nights on his shoulders and the Britons were victorious'.

Some elements in this record are at first sight ridiculous. We may, however, take it that 'three days and three nights' is a literary expression for a protracted battle, such as Gildas's expression 'siege' suggests. What Arthur carried 'on his shoulders' was probably an amulet with a relic of the True Cross. There is no reason to doubt that Badon was an actual battle, in which Arthur was the British commander. But when did it take place? Gildas, having told us that it was in the year of his birth, does not say when that occurred. The British Easter Annals use a reckoning all of their own, from Year 1 to Year 533. It is possible, however, by picking out events which are known from other documents, to calibrate the Annals; and on this basis we can say that 'Year 72' equals AD 518.

Unfortunately this date cannot be reconciled with certain other reckonings. Gildas wrote forty-three years after Badon, so $518 + 43 = $ AD 561. At the time he wrote, Maelgwn was still ruler of north-west Wales, for he was one of the kings whom Gildas denounced. But the British Easter Annals tell us that Maelgwn himself died in AD 549. One at least of these figures must be wrong: can we detect which it is?

The answer lies in a further consideration of the character of Easter Tables. Modern tables, like that, for instance, in the Book of Common Prayer, have *Anno Domini* dates in their left-hand column, and this has been the practice for well over a thousand years. But the system of AD dates, so familiar to us, was not invented until AD 525; so when we find such dates applied to events before then, they have been calculated from figures which had originally been expressed in terms of some other era. Badon, of course, is in this category.

Now early Easter Tables sometimes covered a period of nineteen years only. The reason for this is that the date of Easter is governed by the phases of the moon, and nineteen years is a lunar cycle. It is probable that Badon was originally entered in a nineteen year table, with no further indication of date. Subsequently, some monk with historical interests copied the Badon entry into a table covering a longer span. But he misidentified the lunar cycle, and placed the battle exactly nineteen years too late.

If this is so, then Badon should not be placed at year 72 of the British Easter Annals, AD 518, but at year 53, AD 499. To check this, we add 43 for Gildas's lifetime, to arrive at AD 442 for the time when he was writing, seven years before Maelgwn's death in AD 449.

Fig. 32

Although we can fix the date of Badon with reasonable certainty, there is no agreement as to where it was fought. Identifications which have been suggested include Badbury Rings in Dorset, and Badbury by Liddington Castle in Wiltshire, but neither of these is convincing. Gildas's first-hand knowledge was limited to a tight arc from north Wales to Cornwall and it is likely that Badon was on the periphery of that arc. This makes the medieval identification with Bath very probable, and the 'siege of mount Badonicus' possibly involved one of the hills overlooking that city. There is at least general agreement that it was fought against the Anglo-Saxons in southern England.

1   Smith, L. T., *The itinerary of John Leland in or about the years 1535–1543*, vol. I (London 1907), p. 151. For the early antiquaries, Kendrick, T. D., *British antiquity* (London 1950; reprint, New York and London 1970).

2   Translated from Leland's original Latin by Robinson, R., *The assertion of king Arthure* (London 1582), f. 10 verso; accessible in *Early English text society*, original series 165 (1925 for 1923), 2nd part, p. 35.

3   Stukeley, W., *Itinerarium curiosum* (2nd edn, 1776), centuria I, pl. 43.

4   Stukeley, *Itiner. curios.*, p. 150.

5   Jones, T., 'A sixteenth century version of the Arthurian cave legend', in *Studies in language and literature in honour of Margaret Schlauch* (Warsaw 1966), pp. 175–85.

6   Camden, W., *Britannia* (London 1586), p. 153.

7   Henderson, C., *The Cornish church guide and parochial history of Cornwall* (Truro 1925), p. 57.

8   Pickford, C. E., 'Camelot', *Bibliographical bulletin of the international Arthurian society*, 21 (1969), pp. 158–9.

9   Vinaver, E. (ed.), *The works of Sir Thomas Malory* (3 vols, 2nd edn Oxford 1967), vol. I, p. cxlv.

10   Jones, T., 'The early evolution of the legend of Arthur', *Nottingham Medieval studies*, 8 (1964), pp. 3–21.

11   Alcock, L., *Arthur's Britain: history and archaeology AD 367–634* (London 1971).

12   Note 4 above.

13   Bennett, J. A., 'Camelot', *Proceedings, Somersetshire archaeological and natural history society*, 36 (1890) part 2, pp. 1–19.

14   Gray, H. St G., 'Trial excavations at Cadbury Castle, S. Somerset, 1913', *Proc. Somerset arch. & nat. hist. soc.*, 59 (1913) pt 2, pp. 1–24.

15   Radford, C. A. R., 'Imported pottery found at Tintagel, Cornwall', in Harden, D. B. (ed.), *Dark-age Britain* (London 1956), pp. 59–70.

16   Radford, C. A. R. and Cox, J. S., 'Cadbury Castle, South Cadbury', *Proc. Somerset arch. & nat. hist. soc.*, 99–100 (1954–55), pp. 106–13.

17   For the sceptical view: Treharne, R. F., *The Glastonbury legends* (London 1967). For the contrary view, Radford, C. A. R., 'Glastonbury abbey', in Ashe, G. (ed.), *The quest for Arthur's Britain* (London 1968), pp. 119–38.

18   Harfield, M., 'Cadbury Castle', *Proc. Somerset arch. & nat. hist. soc.*, 106 (1962), pp. 62–5.

19   Howell, M., 'A soil conductivity meter', *Archaeometry*, 9 (1966), pp. 20–3.

20   Aitken, M., 'Magnetic location', and Clark, A., 'Resistivity surveying', in Brothwell, D. and Higgs, E. (eds.), *Science in archaeology* (London 1963; 2nd edn 1969), pp. 681–707.

21   Note 14 above.

22   Windmill Hill: Smith, I. F., *Windmill Hill and Avebury* (Oxford 1965). Maiden Castle: Wheeler, R. E. M., *Maiden Castle, Dorset* (London 1943). Hembury: accessible account in Fox, A., *South West England* (London 1964), pp. 30–2. The main general account is still Piggott, S., *The neolithic cultures of the British Isles* (Cambridge 1954).

23   Houlder, C. H., 'A neolithic settlement on Hazard Hill, Totnes', *Transactions, Devon Archaeological Exploration Society*, new series 21 (1963), pp. 2–31.

24   Accessible account of C-14 dating: Willis, E. H., 'Radiocarbon dating', in *Science in archaeology* (note 20 above), pp. 46–57. For discussion of some of the limitations, *Philosophical Transactions, Royal Society of London*, A 269 (1970), pp. 1–185.

25   Renfrew, C., 'The tree-ring calibration of radio-carbon: an archaeological evaluation', *Proc. Prehist. Soc.*, 36 (1970), pp. 280–311.

26   Hawkes, C. F. C. and Clarke, R. R., 'Gahlstorf and Caister-on-Sea: two finds of Late Bronze Age Irish gold', in Foster, I. Ll.

and Alcock, L., *Culture and environment* (London 1963), pp. 193–250.

27 Musson, C. R., 'House-plans and prehistory', *Current Archaeology*, 2, no. 10 (July 1970), pp. 267–75.

28 Mackie, E., 'Radiocarbon dates and the Scottish Iron Age', *Antiquity*, 43 (1969), pp. 15–26; Savory, H. N., 'A Welsh bronze age hillfort', *Antiquity*, 45 (1971), pp. 251–61. It goes without saying that the C-14 dates quoted in these two papers are as subject to manipulation as any other such dates.

29 Sandars, N. K., *Bronze age cultures in France* (Cambridge 1957), especially fig. 73. Kossak, G., *Südbayern während der Hallstattzeit* (2 vols, Berlin 1959), taf. 9 and 136.

30 Déchelette, J., *Manuel d'archéologie préhistorique, celtique et gallo-romaine. Vol. 3, premier âge du fer ou époque de Hallstatt* (Paris 1913).

31 Brewster, T. C. M., *The excavation of Staple Howe* (Malton 1963).

32 Alcock, L., 'The Irish Sea zone in the pre-Roman Iron Age', in Thomas, C. (ed.), *The Iron Age in the Irish Sea Province* (London 1972), pp. 99–112.

33 Stanford, S. C., 'Credenhill Camp, Herefordshire: an Iron Age hill-fort capital', *Archaeological Journal*, 127 (1970), pp. 82–129.

34 Filip, J., *Celtic civilization and its heritage* (Prague 1960; English edition 1962). Piggott, S., *Ancient Europe* (Edinburgh 1965), pp. 201–7.

35 The best example is Rainsborough: Avery, M., Sutton, J. E. G. and Banks, J. W., 'Rainsborough, Northants., England: excavations, 1961–5', *Proc. Prehist. Soc.*, 33 (1967), pp. 207–306.

36 Compare the undifferentiated fill of the post-pits at Little Woodbury: Bersu, G., 'Excavations at Little Woodbury, Wiltshire, Part 1: the settlement as revealed by excavation', *Proc. Prehist. Soc.*, 6 (1940), pp. 30–111, espec. 78–9.

37 Larger houses: Little Woodbury, note 36. Small houses in forts: Maiden Castle, note 22 above; Hod Hill: Richmond, I. A., *Hod Hill, Vol. II, excavations . . . between 1951 and 1958* (London 1968).

38 For another discussion of these houses, Alcock, L., 'Excavations at Cadbury-Camelot, 1966–70,' *Antiquity*, 46 (1972), pp. 29–38.

39 Latest discussion of grain storage pits: Bowen, H. C., 'Corn storage in antiquity', *Antiquity* 41 (1967), pp. 214–15.

40 Distribution of 'weaving-combs': Henshall, A. S., 'Textiles and weaving appliances in prehistoric Britain', *Proc. Prehist. Soc.*, 16 (1950), pp. 130–62. Caesar's account: *De bello gallico*, V, xiv.

41 I *Samuel* xvii.

42 Full discussion in Allen, D. F., 'Iron currency bars in Britain', *Proc. Prehist. Soc.*, 33 (1967), pp. 307–35.

43 *De bello gallico*, V, xii.

44 This account is based largely on the research of M. G. Spratling.

45 I had originally posed these questions in 1964: 'Hillforts in Wales and the Marches', *Antiquity*, 39 (1965), pp. 184–95.

46 Hod Hill: note 37 above. Caernarvonshire: Royal Commission on Ancient Monuments (Wales), *An inventory of the ancient monuments in Caernarvonshire* (3 vols, London 1956–64). Also Hogg, A. H. A., 'Garn Boduan and Tre'r Ceiri', *Archaeological Journal*, 117 (1960), pp. 1–39.

47 Recent general account of the period: Frere, S. S., *Britannia, a history of Roman Britain* (London 1967).

48 Suetonius, *Divus Vespasianus*, 4.

49 Notes 22 and 37 above.

50 For tribal areas: Ordnance Survey, *Map of southern Britain in the Iron Age* (Chessington 1962); also Rivet, A. L. F., *Town and country in Roman Britain* (London 1958), pp. 151–6.

51 Camulodunum: Hawkes, C. F. C. and Hull, M. R., *Camulodunum: first report on the excavations at Colchester 1930–39* (London 1947) pls. lxxxix–xcvii. Hod Hill: Brailsford, J. W., *Hod Hill, Vol. I, antiquities from Hod Hill in the Durden collection* (London 1962), figs 6–10.

52 There are pointers in Hatt, J-J., *Celts and Gallo-Romans* (London 1970), p. 169; Böhme, A., 'Englische Fibeln aus den Kastellan Saalburg und Zugmantel', *Saalburg Jahrbuch*, 27 (1970), pp. 5–20.

53 For comments on these coins I am indebted to P. J. Casey.

54 I am grateful to G. Dannell for his report on the Samian.

55 Wainwright, G. J., 'The excavation of a Durotrigian farmstead near Tollard Royal in Cranborne Chase, southern England', *Proc. Prehist. Soc.*, 34 (1968), pp. 102–47.

56 Note 22, pp. 61–4, 231–3.

57 Calkin, J. B., 'An early Romano-British kiln at Corfe Mullen, Dorset', *Antiquaries Journal*, 15 (1935), pp. 42–55.

58 General account of Celtic coins; Mack, R. P., *The coinage of ancient Britain* (London 1953; 2nd edn 1964). Distribution maps by Allen, D. F. in OS *Map of southern Britain*, note 50 above. For a critical study, Collis, J. R., 'Functional and theoretical interpretations of British coinage', *World Archaeology*, 3 (1971–2), pp. 71–84.

59 Coins of Dobunni: Allen, D. F., 'A study of the Dobunnic coinage', in Clifford, E. M., *Bagendon: a Belgic oppidum* (Cambridge 1961), pp. 75–149.

60 I am grateful to Professors J. M. C. Toynbee, S. S. Frere and D. E. Strong for their comments on this plaque.

61 Lydney: Wheeler, R. E. M. and Wheeler, T. V., *Report on the excavation of the prehistoric, Roman and post-Roman site in Lydney Park, Gloucestershire* (London 1932). Maiden Castle, note 22 above. Brean Down: Ap Simon, A. M., 'The Roman temple on Brean Down, Somerset', *Proceedings, University of Bristol Spelaeological Society*, 10 (1965), pp. 195–258. General account: Lewis, M. J. T., *Temples in Roman Britain* (Cambridge 1966). For letters comparable with the Cadbury example, Lydney, p. 102 and pl. xxxiv.

62 Leland: note 1 above. Stukeley: note 4.

63 I am grateful to the excavators for information about these key sites in advance of publication.

64 The primary study by Radford (note 15 above) should now be supplemented by Thomas, A. C., 'Imported pottery in dark-age western Britain', *Medieval archaeology*, 3 (1959), pp. 89–111; and by notes in Alcock, *Arthur's Britain*, pp. 201–9.

65 Roman timber gates: Richmond, I. A., 'Roman timber building', in Jope, E. M. (ed.), *Studies in building history* (London 1961), pp. 15–26.

66 Uslar, R. von, *Studien zu frühgeschichtlichen Befestigungen zwischen Nordsee und Alpen* (Köln 1964), pp. 16–33.

67 Alcock, L., 'Castle Tower, Penmaen: a Norman ringwork in Glamorgan', *Antiquaries Journal*, 46 (1966), pp. 178–210, especially pp. 187–90.

68 Examples are the south gate of Hod Hill auxiliary fort: note 37 above, fig. 41 B; and Great Casterton, same report, fig. 50.

69 Castle Dore: Radford, C. A. R., 'Report on the excavations at Castle Dore', *Journal, Royal Institution of Cornwall*, new series 1 (1951), appendix. Yeavering: Colvin, H. M. (ed.), *The history of the king's works* (Vols. I & II, London 1963), pp. 2–5. Cheddar: Rahtz, P. A., 'The Saxon and medieval palaces at Cheddar, Somerset—an interim report of excavations in 1960–62', *Medieval archaeology*, 6–7 (1962–3), pp. 53–66. The hall of Brasenose College, Oxford, is 49 by 25 feet, a floor area of 1225 square feet. The larger room at Cadbury has a floor area of about 1190 square feet if allowance is made for the possibility of a 5 feet wide passage beside the partition, or 1320 square feet without allowing for a passage.

70 Alcock, 'Some reflections on early Welsh society and economy', *Welsh History Review*, 2 (1964–65), pp. 1–7.

71 Alcock, *Dinas Powys* (Cardiff 1963).

72 Castle Dore: note 69 above. Degannwy: Alcock, 'Excavations at Degannwy Castle, Caernarvonshire, 1961–6', *Archaeological Journal*, 124 (1967), pp. 190–201.

73 General survey of Arthurian-period forts: Alcock, *Arthur's Britain*, pp. 209–27, 347–9.

74 Size and organization of armies: *Arthur's Britain*, pp. 335–8.

75 Site of Badon: *Arthur's Britain*, pp. 67–71.

76 Settlement of upper Thames valley: Myres, J. N. L., *Anglo-Saxon pottery and the settlement of England* (Oxford 1969).

77 Accessible translations of the *Anglo-Saxon Chronicle* are by Garmonsway, G. N. (Everyman Library 1953); and by Whitelock, D. with Douglas, D. C. and Tucker, S. I. (London 1961).

78 For the Vikings: Jones, G., *A history of the Vikings* (Oxford 1968).

79 For *burhs* and mints: Loyn, H. R., *Anglo-Saxon England and the Norman Conquest* (London 1962), chapter 3. Radford, C. A. R., 'The later pre-Conquest boroughs and their defences', *Medieval archaeology*, 14 (1970), pp. 83–103, describes the wider background of Cadanbyrig.

80 A well-illustrated introduction is Dolley, R. H. M., *Anglo-Saxon Pennies* (London 1964).

81 Dolley, R. H. M., 'The emergency mint of Cadbury', *British Numismatic Journal*, 28 (1955–7), pp. 99–105.

82 Hill, D., 'The Burghal Hidage: the establishment of a text', *Medieval archaeology*, 13 (1969), pp. 84–92.

83 Case for a church: *Antiquaries Journal*, 48 (1968), pp. 12–3. Reconstruction: *Antiquity*, 42 (1968), p. 49.

84 Colvin, H. M. (ed.), *The history of the king's works* (Vols. I & II, London 1963), p. 583. I am grateful to D. J. C. King for urging on me the reasons for identifying the *castrum de Cadebir* with our site.

85 Alcock, *Arthur's Britain*.

86 Dinas Powys: note 71 above.

87 The primary documents are reproduced in *Arthur's Britain,* especially fig. 3, and are discussed in chapters 2 and 3. The present account supersedes the chronological arguments advanced there, which are unnecessarily elaborate.

List of Illustrations

Unless otherwise stated, the photographs were taken by members of the Cadbury excavation team on film donated by Kodak Ltd, and are the copyright of the Camelot Research Committee. Other photographs are by: Ewart Needham, 1; H. C Tilzey, 3; Royal Naval Air Service, Crown Copyright reserved, 4, 5; H. J. P. Arnold, 6; Associated Press, 14, 40; Aly Aviation, 16, 17; Colin Jeffrey, 26; M. G. Spratling, 51; British Museum, 52; Peter Clayton, 56, 58, 60, 61, 62, 63, 64, 65, 66, 72, 80; XII; Oxford University, Institute of Archaeology, 57; National Museum of Wales, 70, 71; University College, Cardiff, 10, 11, 22, 23, 24, 37, 50, 59, 91, 92, VIII, IX, X, XIII, XIV, XV. Figures 1, 2, 31, 32, 36 were drawn by G. Stephenson; 4, 5, 9–11 by D. Honour; 6, 8 by C. R. Musson; 13–17, 20, 24, 28 by S. Leek; 23 by S. Schotten; 25, 34 by K. D. Howes; 26, 29 by D. L. Owen; all others are by the author.

Figures

Index